# Introduction

I DON'T know how lucky any one person can be but I must be pretty high up on the good fortune tree. I have spent a whole lifetime living my dream of riding motorcycles and, although I have no great ability, I have been in the saddle of some of the best and most exotic motorcycles built.

Despite spending a small fortune on bikes, and having a season ticket at many A&E units up and down the country, I smile just thinking about my good luck: it has been incredible.

I have written for Mortons Media for many years and occasionally go across to their Lincolnshire headquarters to see the book division publisher, Steve O'Hara. Steve is not a motorcyclist, but every time we meet I tell him about this or that fabulous bike – and he is always politely interested.

In the end, he asked me to write a book just about Classic Superbikes. No second-rate machines – however worthy, no nearly great motorcycles and no 'grey porridge'.

Sensible writers, and no-one could ever accuse me of being sensible where bikes are involved, can do all the balanced 'let's-see-both-sides-of-the-coin' stories. No, all the bikes in this book are machines about which I have dreamed – fabulous, loin-tingling, super-duper motorcycles, which get me on the edge of my chair just thinking about them.

Incredibly, at least from my point of view, I have ridden them all, too. I'll share my experiences of being there because these are not marque histories, but what it's actually like to open the throttle of bikes that are so legendary they are almost mythical.

I do hope you enjoy the stories and you think they are, truly, Classic Superbikes.

I also wanted to include a couple of events that have stayed in my memory just because they're so good. At the top of the list had to be Mike Hailwood's 1978 Formula 1 TT win – a success so unlikely it had to be a fictional epic – but wasn't!

I've also included a piece about Retro Moto St Cergue because it encapsulates everything I love about bikes. It's an utterly unreasonable event – noisy, dangerous and impractical. However, what can be more fun than tearing up a Swiss Alp on a race bike and then having a big party afterwards?

Or you could play a video game or visit a garden centre or...

No, Retro Moto is the real deal.

**Author and Concept:** Frank Melling **Editor and Photography:** Carol Melling
**Archive Images:** Jane Skayman **Production Editor:** Nigel Devereux
**Publisher:** Steve O'Hara **Publishing Director:** Dan Savage
**Commercial Director:** Nigel Hole
**Printed by:** William Gibbons and Sons, Wolverhampton **Published by:** Mortons Media Group Ltd, Media Centre, Morton Way, Horncastle, Lincolnshire, LN9 6JR. Tel: 01507 529529
**ISBN:** 978-1-911639-20-6 @ 2020 Mortons Media Group Ltd

# Making Classic Superbikes

If I have been lucky when it comes to riding bikes I have been just as fortunate in working for Mortons Media. As I have mentioned, Steve O'Hara pressed the big green 'go' button for Classic Superbikes and it was great to have Morton's Magazines' managing director Dan Savage on board too. Thanks to you both.

The book has been designed by Michael Baumber and Kelvin Clements, and this is the fourth we have produced together – and they are still working with me, which I guess shows something about how we get on.

The commercial content has been the responsibility of Leon Currie, another long-time collaborator.

The ever-helpful Jane Skayman has found some great pictures from Mortons' magnificent archive, which is unquestionably the best repository of classic motorcycling images in the world. Thanks Jane.

Finally, and most importantly, my wife Carol has toiled on the text until it is the very best we can make it. As husband and wife we get on very well but when she's the editor and I am an author, discussions can sometimes get awfully near a mixed martial arts' bout!

Additionally, Carol took almost all of the pictures in this book–and she's a brilliant race mechanic, too. And no, she doesn't have a twin sister who's looking for a long-term relationship with a classic bike racer.

I would like to conclude by thanking all of the many people who have entrusted me with their valuable bikes over the years. I want to begin with the legendary Sammy Miller, and the Sammy Miller Motorcycle Museum, for letting me ride his Gilera 4 – the bike that has been with me all my life.

Next, all of the organisers at Retro Moto St Cergue in Switzerland – as much fun as you can have in a day without an irate dad complaining to your mum about his daughter!

Ben Walker, at Bonham's Auctions, has been brilliant. Ben has forgotten more about classic bikes than I will ever know.

Then there is Fritz Egli - and Alex Frei - for letting me ride the Egli Fritz: what a bike!

Dave Brown, a private owner, extended the great privilege of letting me try his utterly original Ducati 900SS and Steve Wynne, the man behind Mike Hailwood's incredible 1978 TT win, told me the true and accurate story behind the success.

Stuart Wood and Miles Perkins at Triumph were endlessly patient in giving me the background to the Street Twin, which has proved to be such a whopping sales success in the retro market. Ron Willis was kind enough to lend me his Hesketh Venom so I could feel what it was like to be a real two-wheeled aristocrat for a few hours.

My long-time friend Clive Brooker somehow wangled me a ride on a real, ex-Ron Haslam CB1100R, and I got to ride the machine at Spa-Francorchamps. What an honour!

Lawrence Rose, of Classic Motorcycles in Cheshire, is always helpful and lets me ride all sorts of exotica that he has in stock – which shows a lot of faith. Thanks Lawrence.

Finally, thanks to the National Motorcycle Museum and James Hewing for allowing me to have a proper go on 'Slippery Sam', the most famous production racer of all time.

Norman Hyde was incredibly helpful in terms of the background to the bike as was the man who built it, Les Williams, who has now sadly passed away.

As you can see, a lot of people trust in my ability not to go grass tracking on their very precious machines. Thanks to you all.

MOTO GUZZI

DUCATI

Best wishes
Jack Melling
Christmas
2022

# Contents

# Gilera Four

## The Best of the Best of the Best

"The Gilera got me caned by Mr Sharman – and I hope the fiends of hell are treating you in an appropriately severe manner, Sir – for drawing the exquisite double overhead cam engine on the very last, tatty page of my jotter"

I want to begin this book with a really impressive, show-stopping bike, so I have chosen the 1957 Gilera Four. There were many reasons for doing this. First, the Gilera was outstandingly the most successful bike during the Golden Age of Grand Prix motorcycle racing – the period when a myriad of factories competed with everything from single-cylinder two-strokes through to eight-cylinder four-strokes. The only thing missing was the dull uniformity of current GP racing, where every bike is a four-cylinder four-stroke!

The Gilera is also one of the most perfectly beautiful motorcycles ever made – although its designers only had function, not form, in mind. Then the bike got me caned by Mr Sharman – and I hope that the fiends of hell are treating you in an appropriately severe manner, Sir – for drawing the exquisite double overhead cam engine on the very last, tatty page of my jotter on the final day of term.

But, most of all, if ever a motorcycle can be described as having anthropomorphic properties, it is the Gilera. Just rolling up to the start line was like controlling an eager stallion.

Although I never saw an original Gilera Four race, it's a bike which has been with me all my life, and is woven into my motorcycling DNA.

It was a big effort for my parents to find the money, but for my 12th birthday I was given a Dansette record player. In the red, vinyl-covered box there was a turntable and, at the front, a small, built-in speaker controlled by knurled, plastic knobs. It was a symbol that I was growing up and ready to become part of the rock 'n' roll generation.

My mum bought me the Beatles' I Wanna Hold Your Hand, and my avant-garde older cousin gave me a quite badly scratched, long play vinyl record from the film GI Blues, and I sang along with Elvis and Wooden Heart as I did my homework.

But my parents failed in their noble attempt to both civilise and convert me into a mainstream teenager, for I had a secret sin. No – not illegal drugs which, in my small, industrial town in the north of England, hadn't been invented yet.

Nor was it looking at partially undressed ladies in magazines which were only sold to grown-ups from secret supplies under the counter.

No, my addiction had come from the second-hand shop which was located just next to the railway bridge, opposite the Horse and Jockey pub. In there, for the princely sum of two shillings and six pence (12½p) – a whole week's pocket money – I bought a well-worn copy of the Stanley Schofield recordings from the 1957 TT.

And so I would go into my bedroom, close the door tight, put the Dansette under my bed sheets and, in the claustrophobic darkness, listen to the wailing, siren call of Bob McIntyre winning the 1957 Golden Jubilee TT on his four-cylinder Gilera.

The crackle of the British singles was the heart and body of Grand Prix racing in motorcycling's golden era, but the warbling wail of the four-cylinder Gilera was more than this–it touched my soul. My 1960s monochrome world was rent asunder by the technicolour ululation of the Gilera's war song, which scarred my young brain forever.

There is an old adage that you should never, ever meet your heroes, and so it was with a real sense of trepidation that I sat on Sammy Miller's Gilera Four and received a briefing from Sam's super mechanic, John Ring.

To be blunt, John was not overwhelmingly happy I was being allowed to ride the bike. In fact, other than Sam, I am the only rider to have been allowed to use it. World champions, media superstars and biking celebrities have been permitted to sit on the bike, as I have done many times in the past at bike shows and gatherings – but only with the engine cold and lifeless.

Now, John has warmed up the Gilera and I am a few minutes away from riding it.

The briefing begins. "The engine is very free revving and it will spin on until it blows up. That's what happened in New Zealand when Sam got too enthusiastic.

"Change gear at 8,500 rpm and don't let it go anywhere near 10,000 or you will destroy it.

"Don't let the engine go below 5,000rpm either. It will pull from nothing but the crank doesn't like very low revs.

"Don't be rough with the clutch. These bikes were never made for clutch starts so the clutch sits on a very shallow spline and you'll break it if you're rough. Don't break it! ▸

**1**
**The iconic Gilera Four engine – the most successful, and beautiful, Grand Prix motor of its day. I got caned for drawing one in my jotter. Some teachers have no culture!**

**2**
**Coming to the line with a lot of concentration. They don't sell spares for Gilera Fours at your local Pound Shop.**

**3**
**Tucked in, throttle cable stretched tight and living the dream. The Gilera Four was too precious NOT to ride flat out!**

**4**
**L-R The Gilera's guardian, John Ring. Me – looking as happy as if I'd just achieved my life-long dream, and Sammy – still smiling because the bike is in one piece.**

❷

❸

❹

**1.**
**The orchestra which played music for my soul.**

**2.**
**1955 TT. The bike on the right has the new dustbin fairing and the two others have the older, bikini fairing.** MORTONS MEDIA GROUP LTD

**3.**
**Bob McIntyre in full flight over Ballaugh Bridge, as he wins the 1957 TT at an average speed of 98.99 mph.** MORTONS NICK NICHOLLS COLLECTION

"Be careful with the front brake. There is a powerful, self-servo effect and the front will lock in a flash.

"The rear wheel will, too. Don't lock the brakes.

"If you crash it, don't even think about coming back..."

It's not so much the Gilera's £100,000 value which concerns John, but rather the horrendous logistical consequences of an accident – or even a mechanical problem. You just don't phone your local bike shop and have them ship out replacement parts for a 1957 Gilera Grand Prix bike for next day delivery.

Miller's bike is interesting in a huge variety of ways. The absolute facts are it is not an authentic Gilera Four, but one of six replicas which were built by Mark and Dave Kay of Meccanica Verghera Engineering – somewhat ironically based in Walsall, in the heart of Britain's engineering and manufacturing Midlands.

The Kays are nothing short of genius: no other word adequately describes their ability. The two of them are probably responsible for keeping more classic race bikes on the track than any other people in the world.

Dave explains: "A customer brought us a 1952 Gilera for repair and we really liked the bike. It was one of the legendary motorcycles of all time and we enjoyed working on it.

"Later on, the same customer brought us a 1957 Gilera Four, which was the last model the factory produced, and was the ultimate example of all Gilera's race bikes.

"We came to an arrangement whereby we could copy the bike and make a small number of replicas.

He continues: "From the start, we wanted to make a bike which was an absolute clone of the original bike. We could have easily improved it, in the same way in which many British racing singles have been modernised to increase performance. But we were determined to make machines that were absolutely identical to the original bikes. This means that what was good on the original bikes is good on our machines and what was bad stays bad.

"We know we got things right because we keep a lot of the original Gileras in Italy on the track, using our parts.

"Making a Gilera Four is every bit as difficult as you would imagine. The job was particularly challenging because the bike we had to copy was incomplete. We had to get inside the minds of designer Franco Passoni and the Gilera race team, and work out what they intended to do rather than just use modern techniques to solve the questions.

"Once we understood what they had been thinking, the actual manufacturing was extremely demanding. For example, the cylinder head is a nightmare and is made in multiple parts. Through years of living with the bikes, the Gilera staff had come to understand the manufacturing tolerances.

Dave adds: "We had to use our experience to get things right first time and it wasn't easy.

"As well as being exact replicas of the original bikes, we wanted them to be 100% race worthy – not just bits of dead metal to be used as ornaments.

"We achieved this aim too, with Pat Sefton just failing to reach Bob McIntyre's 100mph lap when we raced the 'Four' in the 2005 Manx Grand Prix.

"That bike was sold to fund the MV Agusta project. (Dave is currently manufacturing clones of Agostini's world championship-winning, three-cylinder MV Agusta), but I always have a soft spot for the Gilera, so I am making a new bike for myself."

Gilera's history of racing four-cylinder machines goes all the way back to 1936 when the factory bought the rights to the CNA Rondine, four-cylinder machine. This was the first practical bike to have the cylinders transposed across the

frame in the manner which, much later, the Japanese made the industry standard.

Gilera was owned, and very tightly controlled, by founder Giuseppe Gilera, and he had ambitions to make his company a world leader in motorcycle design and production.

As well as being an astute businessman, Gilera was a talented motorcycle racer and mechanic who understood the potential of the four cylinder engine – and the publicity it could bring to the Arcore factory.

Always retaining an across the frame design for cooling, the Gilera Four underwent many redesigns until it reached its (almost) ultimate form in Kay's re-creation of the five-speed, 1957 design, which gave Bob McIntyre the 500cc World Championship.

The motor was still a two-valve per cylinder design, but the highly talented, and practical, Franco Passoni increased the cylinder bore to 58.8mm with two pairs of cylinder heads. There were four separate cylinder barrels and one long, magnesium cam cover – and the whole lot was bolted to the crankcases via 12 long studs: all very practical if you were a Gilera mechanic in 1957, but a nightmare for the Kays to re-create.

The valves were opened by a gear train because this was considered to be the most reliable method possible with the available technology.

Gears were also used for the primary drive to the clutch, again for reliability, and they feed the power to a five speed gearbox with the classic, right-hand side European gear shift pattern of one up and four down.

A one-gallon oil sump was positioned beneath the engine to help lower the centre of gravity.

In this trim, the motor produced around 70hp and the bike weighed 150kg (330lb). This was 18kg (40lb) heavier than the best Manx Nortons or Matchless G50s – but with a whopping 20hp more than the British singles.

**The immaculate Geoff Duke at the bottom of Bray Hill in the 1955 TT. Duke took all his knowledge of riding the fine handling works Norton to Gilera and transformed the Italian bikes.** MORTONS MEDIA GROUP LTD

"A top quality Manx was good for around 135 mph in contrast with the Gilera which would be nudging 155mph"

A top quality Manx was good for around 135mph – and that was a really world class example – in contrast with the Gilera which would, in the right conditions, be nudging 155mph. Far more importantly, the Gilera would simply slaughter a Manx or G.50 in terms of acceleration.

When Geoff Duke left Norton to join Gilera he took with him an intimate knowledge of the best handling race bike in the world at the time: the Norton 30M Manx.

Geoff made a number of suggestions to bring the Gilera closer to the Norton in terms of handling performance – and a new frame, which lowered the engine and was shorter, became standard. This is the frame used on the Miller bike.

Also used on this bike are the formidable 220mm, double-sided, four-leading shoe front brake and the single-sided, twin-leading shoe rear brake.

It's worth exploding a myth at this point. The truth is that drum brakes can provide epic braking power when compared with a disc. The problem is they are hugely more complex to make; much more difficult to use; and fade more under severe use.

The issue with the Gilera brake is that it has a ferocious self-servo effect. Once the brake shoes bite, the rider has to ease the lever pressure to prevent the front wheel from locking uncontrollably.

With the astonishing levels of grip offered by modern classic race tyres, even an ordinary club rider of my standard can use the power of the brakes, but in 1957 it must have a taken a genius to prevent them locking.

Sammy Miller issued no threats or warnings – just a smile and the instruction: "Go and enjoy yourself."

The test track was perfect for a 1950s GP bike because ▸

it was the narrow, bumpy roads used for the Cholmondeley Pageant of Power – a very good replica of the surfaces on which GPs were run 50 years ago.

The first thing which hits me is how small the Gilera is. Maybe simply because of its reputation, or perhaps the width of those legendary four cylinders, whenever you see the bike at a show there is the feeling that it is a bulky thing. In real life, the opposite is true. It is physically smaller than the Manx Norton, which I was racing at the time, and feels more like our much later Seeley Suzuki.

The ergonomics are superb. Everything falls to hand in the most natural way possible. The clutch is feather light and the bike just begs the rider to get down into a racing crouch. First, last and middle, this is a GP bike – and there is no mistaking the fact.

John hands the Gilera over to me fully warmed up and now it's the moment of truth. Will my mechanical hero prove to be a Disney World illusion made from recycled Chinese plastic?

The throttle is light and the revs soar with the merest hint of throttle. The rev counter needle scorches anti-clockwise round the dial with worrying speed. The old adage is true: there are no atheists on the battlefield. I babble a prayer under my Arai: "Please God, don't let me wreck the bike even before the start line."

I roll the Gilera down to the timing lights with the bike in neutral to protect the fragile clutch. Then, with no fanfare of trumpets, chariots of fire descending from the clouds or any other heavenly sign, the starting light goes green and I have an empty track and control of a legend.

The Gilera wail is much softer and more sonorous than a modern, unsilenced four- cylinder engine. I bring the revs up to 5,500 and then gently ease in the clutch, so that the bike is balanced just on the edge of the power band, and then we are away.

It is impossible not to fall into the racing position and, once I am on the fuel tank, the bike is beautifully balanced. The gears pop in effortlessly, and in seconds I am running at 9,000 rpm – the bottom edge of the GP power band – which is 90mph through Cholmondeley's wooded avenue.

In just a few seconds, I am at home. Rather than being some exotic monster, the Gilera is as friendly and helpful as a working gundog.

Turning left at the end of the Chestnut Avenue, it takes only light pressure to get that huge front brake working, and I am grateful for John's timely advice. Again, what a dream it would be to have a brake like this in a modern classic race.

Out of the hairpin, the Gilera pulls well with the clutch in. Okay, if I were racing I would want to get into the power quicker, but the motor spins up easily and we're off again, head in the tank and trying desperately not to get near racing speeds.

Through the chicane, the Gilera's relaxed steering makes itself known with a reluctance to flick from one angle of lean to the other–but there were no chicanes in 1957 when true road racing ruled the GP world.

Downhill and off-camber at Chapel Bends, the Gilera is rock solid and trustworthy. I catch a glimpse of the Armco on the right and, for a split second, imagine the consequences of getting the left-hander wrong – for me and the bike.

As every yard goes by I get to like the bike more and more until, by the end of the lap, I am beginning to dream terrible, fantasy dreams.

I need two, not one, Gileras. I need one in the original trim so that on every day that is less than perfect I can go across to the workshop, crack it up and feel better about life.

I then need a second Four, silenced to current racing levels so I can race it hard in classic events. If the Gilera is fantastic here, ridden gently and with respect to the bike and its owner, what would it be like at Spa with the back end hanging out at 130mph?

So, if any reader has a spare £200,000 to fulfil a bike junkie's dreams, do let me know. ◆

**AND A POST SCRIPT:**

I gave the bike back to John with a very real sense of relief along with the comments. "Well there we go–back in one piece and no scratches."

John half smiled and commented: "Yes, I know. I was watching you every inch of the way on the big screen TV."

It was just like giving in my homework on time…

With many thanks to Sammy Miller for showing me greater trust than I reasonably deserved.

**Gilera Four – Form and function combined to make motorcycling art.**

Sammy always rides his Gilera hard.

Sammy Miller is one of the great figures in motorcycling history. He was a strong candidate for world championship road racing glory, riding for the Italian FB Mondial team before the factory withdrew from GP racing, leaving the young Miller without a ride.

Sammy was also a brilliant trials rider and was soon a member of the Ariel factory team. With all the confidence and courage of youth, the young Ulsterman relocated to Birmingham, which in 1957 was the heart of the world motorcycle industry, to join Ariel as an employee. There he developed Ariel's ageing 500cc single-cylinder bike into the world's best trials machine.

Bultaco recognised his brilliance not only as a trials rider but also as one of the most free-thinking development engineers of his generation. Miller quite literally designed the Bultaco Sherpa from scratch, and this 250cc two-stroke was to become a huge success throughout the world for the small Spanish factory.

As Bultaco began to struggle against the ever fiercer Japanese opposition Miller was head-hunted again – this time by Honda.

Although still a brilliant rider, Sammy now took on three roles: rider, Honda factory team manager and development designer – and excelled in all three.

Honda went on to dominate trials for 14 outstanding years.

Sammy Miller MBE.

However, there was a glitch in the Miller success story. Honda's vision was that trials would take the American motorcycling scene by storm. They produced superb, easy to ride bikes, and Miller promoted trials on American tours – but all to no avail. Americans never did take to trials in a serious way, and eventually Honda lost interest.

But Sammy was also a very successful motorcycle dealer in his own right and manufacturer of specialist parts for trials bikes.

In parallel with his shop, Sammy became a collector of motorcycles, at first just to fuel his passion for bikes, but now he was able to make this into a yet another full time, world-leading business.

"It started with a few bikes I really liked and fancied owning but I soon needed a bigger garage. Eventually, in 1996, the museum was born and we now have more than 325 machines in one of the world's best collections of exotic bikes."

Sam's contributions to motorcycling were recognised by HM Queen when she made him a Member of the British Empire in 2009 – one of the very few motorcyclists to receive this high honour.

Now, Sammy Miller MBE is a mainstay of the classic motorcycling scene and demonstrates his iconic race bikes throughout the world.

# Retro Moto St Cergue

## What's more fun than hooning up a Swiss Alp on a classic race bike?

Retro Moto is one of the best kept secrets on the international classic motorcycling circuit – and is all the better for this.

There is no glitz, glamour or even much of a trade presence. Instead, there's the chance to ride one of the world's greatest strips of tarmac in the company of 300 hard-core classic enthusiasts, wander round a completely unrestricted paddock, and finish off the day with a celebratory meal. Now, tell me, what's better in life than that?

Retro Moto is held every two years and I have ridden in the event three times - I enjoy it so much. For us, based in the north of England, it's a considerable commitment to take our Seeley Suzuki 900 miles – plus a Channel crossing – but the time, money and effort is amply repaid by the event.

Retro Moto is based in St Cergue – a tiny village, sitting high up in the Vaud Mountains of Switzerland, 22 miles from Geneva. It's worth going to St-Cergue just for the view looking across Lake Geneva to the French Haute-Savoie. However,

**Retro Moto 2017 - Melling allegedly at work on his 500cc Seeley Seeley Suzuki.**

Arai
39

1

although the village is picture-postcard pretty, the key attraction for motorcyclists is that St-Cergue is at the end of the Route de Nyon, which snakes up from the valley below.

At one time, St-Cergue was the finish of a full-on racing hill climb dating back to 1901, when four bikes and 28 cars battled their way up a 10km (6.21 miles) course. Races were held on and off for many years, until 1934, when this historic hill went into retirement.

Then in 2001, over a glass of wine or 10, a group of bike enthusiasts had the idea of running a retrospective event using the same, spectacular stretch of Nyon – St- Cergue road.

The elephant in the, no doubt immaculate, bathroom is that the Swiss have a very schizophrenic attitude towards racing.

As a nation, the Swiss are speed mad and have produced some superstar bike racers over the years. Unfortunately, following a horrendous accident at the 1953 Swiss Grand Prix, in which three spectators were killed, the Swiss government banned all road racing – but, through some bureaucratic quirk, allowed hill climbing to continue.

Not that hill climbs don't bite – as TV's Grand Tour presenter Richard Hammond found out in 2017, when he launched an electric car down a lovely Swiss Alp. Regardless of your skill level, you need to treat these Swiss hills with a lot of respect!

Relaunching the event was helped immensely by the fact Retro Moto is run as a not- for-profit event and any surplus funds go to charity. The last time I rode the hill, Zoe4Life, which supports families where a child has had cancer, were the worthy beneficiaries. Spectator admission to Retro Moto is free of charge, but the understanding is you will chip in a few francs to the charity – which is more than very reasonable.

However, the critical factor in Retro Moto's existence is it is not a timed, speed hill climb. Rather, it is a demonstration of what a timed hill climb might look like if it ever took place at St-Cergue – which clearly it couldn't, and wouldn't, because this would involve going a bit more than rather fast, using all the road and sliding up the inside of slower riders on hairpin bends, which clearly never happened and never would Officer, cross-my-heart-and-hope-to-die-poke-a-needle-in-my-eye-if-I-ever-tell-a-lie...

There is immense goodwill at the event and a wonderful welcome from the village. The organisation is smooth and efficient, but very light touch, and riders join in with the idea that fast is fun, but reckless is silly and should be avoided.

The organisers understand, on a very fundamental level, what makes the event successful. Here's one small, but perfectly formed, example. ▸

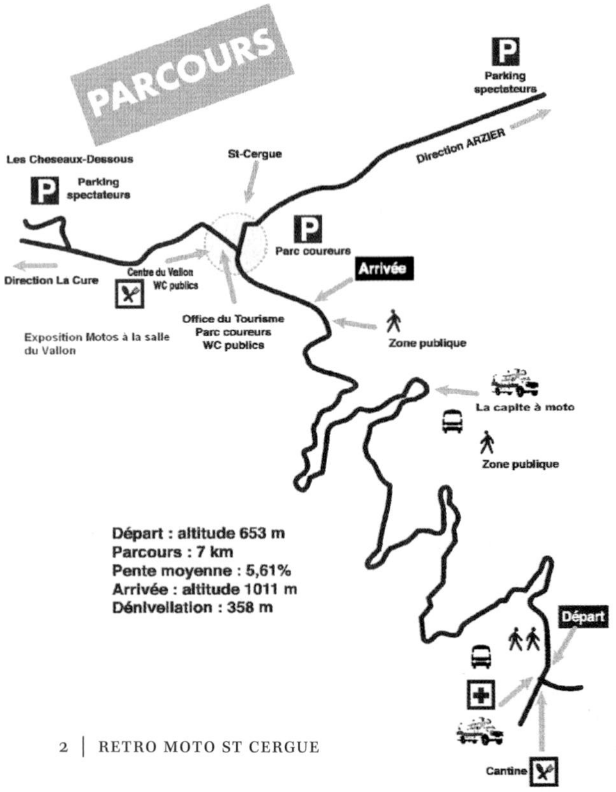


**1**
**Now that does take some confidence. Phillippe Allier hammering 20k of CBX up a Swiss mountain road.**

**2**
**The Swiss have an interesting interpretation of the English word 'demonstration'.**

**3**
**The universal beer tent.**

**4**
**The tiny Swiss village of St Cergue really welcomes Retro Moto.**

❷

③
MOTO - RETRO
BIERE
SAMEDI
29 JUILLET 2017
MOTO-RETRO

④
CALANDA
Rétro Moto Internationale
Saint-Cergue
17 Juin 2017
17 juin 2017
Gingins > Saint-Cergue
• Plus de 250 participants
27 titres mondiaux
10 nations
• 4 montées
• Motos et side-cars
• Grande exposition de motos d'exception
• Parc des coureurs au centre de Saint-Cergue
• Buvettes
• Banquet le samedi soir
• Entrée gratuite
Rétro Moto
Internationale
1ère montée dès 9h00
Départ: Main de Gingins > Arrivée: Point du Jour à St-Cergue
(Tout ou partie du bénéfice va à des œuvres de bienfaisance)
Organisation
Association Rétro Moto Internationale de Saint-Cergue
Infos: www.retro-moto.ch

1

2

During my last visit it was more than a bit hot with the mercury whizzing happily past 34°C – that's a whopping 90°F in old money. The sun hammered down as we waited in the collecting box by the start line, and race leathers looked like something worth avoiding at all costs. Then, along came some smiling officials with gallons of chilled water and an endless supply of disposable glasses. What a lovely, thoughtful, intimate touch.

The descent down the hill is busy, with 300 excited little racers all wanting to get to the start line, but it's also a wonderful experience to ride through the Alpine forest and then come out looking down over Lake Geneva and across to the mountains of the northern French Alps in the far distance – even in summer, still wearing their caps of snow.

This is what makes Retro Moto so special and it is important not to forget just what a privilege we were all enjoying – thanks to the organisers and the goodwill of the local community. Riding our wonderful Suzuki, surrounded by the boom and crackle of hundreds of classic race bikes, in a place so idyllic that it would be beyond anyone's imagination to conceive, certainly made me feel like one very lucky boy.

Then there is the ride up. Oooooohhhhhhh – la montée! I always have difficulty describing just how good this 7km (4.3 miles) of tarmac is to ride. There are something like 46 corners, depending how pedantic you want to be about what is a curve and what is a true bend, ranging from 20mph hairpins to bottom-clenching fast sweeps, where the penalties for getting things wrong are severe.

I have been fortunate to ride racing motorcycles all over the world and the Route de Nyon rates right at the very top of the tree for riding pleasure.

Wannabee GP stars jostle for position on ancient classics as if it is the last lap of this year's MotoGP finale. The mix of bikes is hair-raisingly eclectic. On one side of me is an extremely senior citizen aboard a pre-war Manx Norton and on the other a recently retired World Superstock rider with a very trick 1980s Laverda.

Pottering road bikes share track space with serious ex-grand prix riders on hot post-classic racers. All are here to enjoy what is one of the most satisfying experiences in motorcycling.

The range of motorcycles has shifted over the years. Now, the event is dominated by late classics – some very late indeed – and the riders too are getting ever younger. This is right and proper if the classic motorcycle movement is to stay alive and healthy – and the organisers of Retro Moto are to be commended for allowing the event to drift towards younger bikes and riders who still have a full head of hair and eat with their own teeth.

What I can't understand is so called star riders who have no empathy with classics. The real motorcycling icons like Jim Redman, Jean Claude-Castella, Alain Genoud and the rest of these international stars were very evident and wholly accessible to fans. By contrast, the organisers had brought in some younger riders, on modern bikes, who might just as well have not been there for all the public saw of them. Maybe it's the difference between the kindness and, dare I say it, humility of the classic stars and the way these younger riders view themselves. As six times world champion, and six times TT winner, Jim Redman said: "Chatting to fans isn't a job I avoid – it's a privilege. Without them, I wouldn't be here." ▸

**1**
**A few current GP stars make an appearance at St Cergue. Here's Loris Baz riding a retired Desmosedici – nice, but the real stars are the old bikes.**

**2**
**Putting on a show is a vital part of Retro Moto.**

**3**
**Now that's commitment! Pierre-Alain and the lovely Kilian Murisier, and their immaculate BMW, show what full on demonstrations mean.**

**4**
**Here's how a vintage bike should be ridden. Thierry Martin and his 1926, 350 Chater Lea TT replica.**

①

②

③

And that attitude is what makes not only a great motorcycle racer but a great man, too. Maybe Jim should be leading seminars on greatness...

At the end of the day I was dead on my feet. Five descents, and clearly ascents too, of the hill was a lot of riding and added to this was a compulsory, and lengthy, tour of what was a truly fascinating paddock. But there was still one more challenge left: the celebratory dinner held in St-Cergue's palatial village hall.

Post-race parties can, to put things in the most discreet and modest terms, become more than a little boisterous. Put a couple of hundred racers, still with a lot of post event adrenaline running through their veins, in the company of a generous supply of alcohol and the results are sometimes not edifying.

At Retro Moto, things are very different. Maybe it is because the public can join in the fun so the ratio of racers to normal human beings is diluted. Perhaps the reason lies in the large number of females present but, most probably, the answer lies in the blanket of goodwill and harmony which pervades every molecule of the event. In short, the Retro Moto organisers are just really, really nice people.

We sat with Jim Redman and things were going more

1
Guy Fellay 1979 Honda CBX.

2
Retro Moto attracts a big crowd'.

3
Somewhat amazingly, Alexandre Mischeler's little red BSA Barracuda didn't blow up all day - despite being given a good thrashing.

4
Later classics were popular at Retro Moto. Here's Eric and Joris Bonnefoy giving their Suzuki some stick.

than very well as he told us stories from great times with Honda – and then some deity with a sense of humour decided to have a laugh at my expense! Georges Chatelain, who was then President of Retro Moto's Comité de Direction, and a leading contender for the Nicest Person in Switzerland award, asked would I please say a few words in French to what appeared to be the 10 million people attending the party?

From this experience I learnt three things. First, I should have paid more attention in Miss Pilar's French lessons instead of surreptitiously reading bike mags under my desk. Second, if you think that speaking in public, in English, is hard then you should try it using only paddock French and a smile. Finally, not getting booed or having lumps of bread thrown at me at the end of two minutes was better than winning MotoGP!

Retro Moto St-Cergue happens only every other year so you'll have to keep a close watch for when it is on. If you can find it, then it is certainly worth a visit. ◆

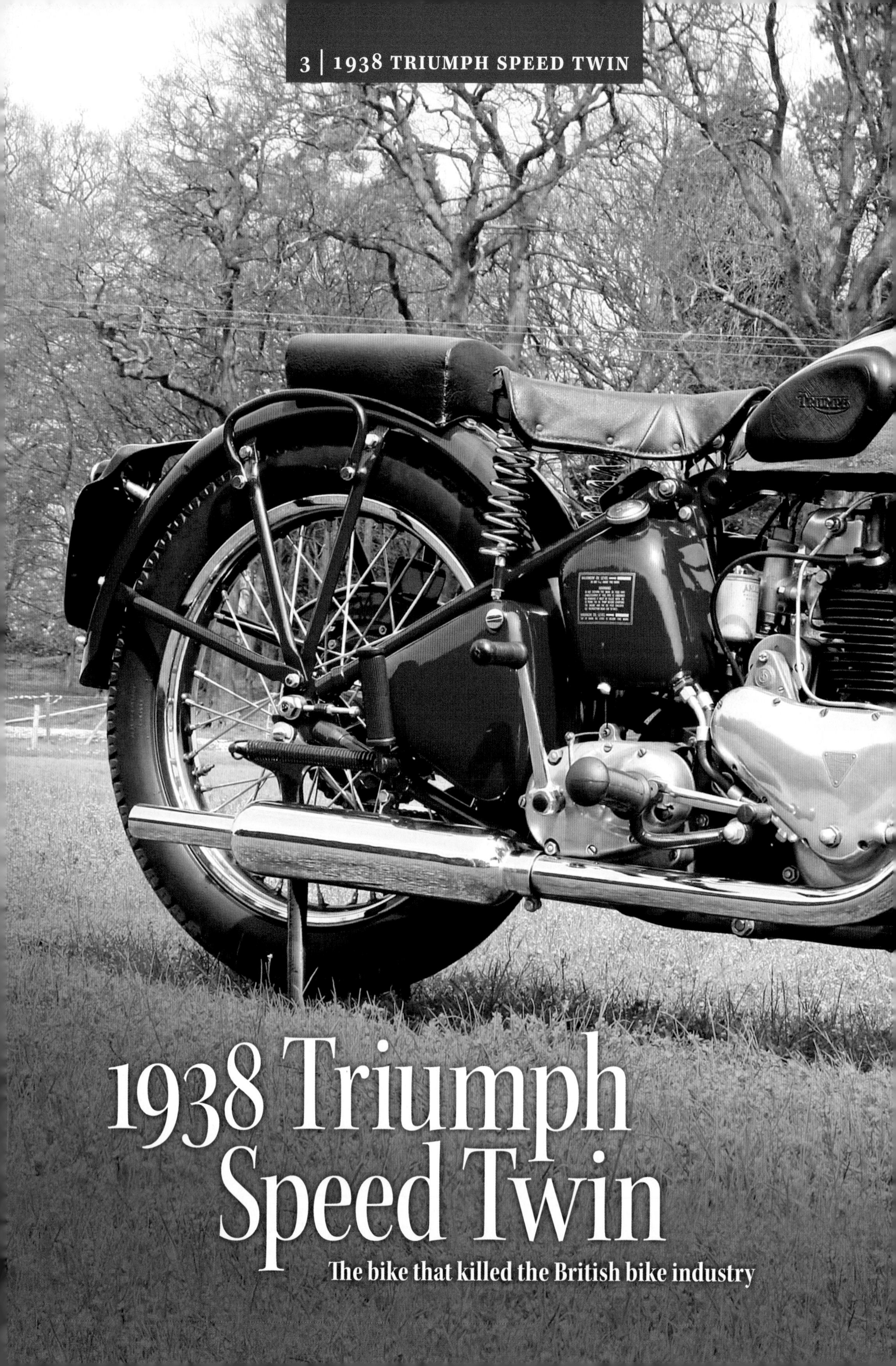


# 1938 Triumph Speed Twin

## The bike that killed the British bike industry

TRIUMPH
CVF 348

The first Triumph Speed Twin is a motorcycle that really tugs at my heart strings. In 1938, my parents were, very much, an upwardly mobile working class couple – well paid and living life to the full.

My mum was very beautiful, with cascades of burnished, pale red hair and the smile on my dad's face in 1938 is full of self-confidence.

He was a valued customer at Jack Frodsham Motorcycles, the Triumph agent in Warrington, and when the revolutionary new Triumph Speed Twin hit the market the demand was such that just a favoured few were allowed to own one: my dad did.

This elite group of high-spending customers had to put a walloping £75 on the table, cash up front – a lot of money, when a skilled person like my dad was earning around £3 10s (£3.50) a week before tax. Comparatively, that's more expensive than the top spec Triumph Thruxton R currently sells at.

Both my parents loved their bike and, the following year, they part-exchanged it for the brand new, and even more exotic, bronze-headed Tiger 100 – again, a machine for customers at the very top of the priority tree. They had the bike for only a few months before my dad joined the Navy and went to war. I would love to know what happened to that Tiger 100 – which disappeared at just a couple of months old!

So I have always wanted a Speed Twin – to reach back into those wonderful, pre-war days when my parents were idyllically happy and war seemed impossible. Unfortunately, when I have been in a position where I could afford a Speed Twin there was never quite the right bike available. Conversely, when there was the dream machine, there wasn't the money.

Instead, I have ridden lots of these pre-war twins and they really are a remarkably sweet motorcycle – and not over hyped. Equally, they were the poisoned chalice that not only destroyed Triumph but the rest of the British motorcycle industry, too.

The 1938 Triumph Speed Twin is one of the most important motorcycles of all time and if ever a machine needs to be put into context it is this one. The Speed Twin, almost on its own, took Triumph from the edge of bankruptcy to being one of the most important motorcycle manufacturers in the world, while simultaneously sowing the seeds of the marque's eventual demise.

The Speed Twin's creator, Edward Turner, enjoyed so much success with his bike, and its later siblings, he was allowed to run Triumph in an utterly autocratic, not to say narcissistic, manner. This was bad management practice and, later, Triumph were to pay a terrible price.

The Speed Twin also inculcated the idea in British manufacturers' boardrooms that if you were smart, or what appeared to be smart, you could avoid investment in R&D and new models. This mind set was also to cost the British dear in the 1960s.

Conceptually, the Speed Twin was quintessentially Japanese, in that it was a user- friendly product which had mass market appeal. Had the British remembered the lessons of the first Speed Twin then it is highly likely the Japanese manufacturers would still be confined to the Far East. In short, the Speed Twin is a keystone in the history of motorcycling.

Firstly, we need to think of the historical context in which the Speed Twin made its appearance in 1937. This was the era following the Great Depression, which had killed off so much of the nascent motorcycle manufacturing industry in Britain – and the rest of the world, too. Having committed commercial suicide through excessive diversification, Triumph had been bought out of bankruptcy by John 'Jack' Sangster ,who owned Ariel Motorcycles. Sangster only managed to pull off this deal through some rather cute manoeuvring at asset disposal sales, as well as being very well connected in the Midlands' motor parts industry.

In the late-1930s, there were some very fine motorcycles in production, but the market leaders were predominantly sporting singles. A high-performance single is still a wonderful animal for the hard core, sporting rider, and there were some excellent bikes on sale. Excelsior had the Manxman, Rudge their iconic Ulster – with its fabulously exotic, bronze cylinder head – and Norton would, subject to the factory's erratic production, sell you an International with a genuine 100mph performance.

The problem was these cutting-edge bikes were suitable only for the enthusiast. They were all expensive to make and ▸

**1**
**Lithe, graceful, practical, efficient – and easy to build. At the start, Turner's creation was pure genius.**

**2**
**The Speed Twin engine was easy to build, reliable and user friendly. It could have been the start of something wonderful for the British Bike Industry'.**

"Edward Turner was blessed with an uncanny knack of knowing exactly what made motorcyclists buy bikes."

❷

demanded a lot of maintenance. They were even challenging to start without a high level of skill! Everyone in the pub claimed that they wanted a Norton 'Inter' – but few spent their precious wage packets on buying a bike.

Move down a level to more affordable machines and the prospective buyers were faced with a wall-to-wall selection of worthy, but dull, bikes. Black was the standard colour, and machines like the Matchless G90, while sound enough motorcycles, did nothing to get the blood racing.

So this is the stage on to which the Speed Twin is about to make its debut. Now, what of the bike's creator? Bert Hopwood, a contemporary of Turner's, and later to be head of BSA, referred to him thus: "He was quite definitely the most egotistical man I have ever met..."

Hopwood, himself one of Britain's leading – if not most successful – designers, then went on to say: "As an engineer, Edward Turner seemed to lack the technical knowledge that must be embraced if engineering design is to be anything but guesswork.

"Indeed, he dismissed as 'academics' most of the people whose job it was to make sure, by mathematics, that the company's (Triumph) products had reasonable factors of safety.

"However, he was an inventive genius and had a flair for pleasing shapes and an uncanny ability to 'smell out' what the buying public would readily accept."

Hopwood's summary was a very fair representation of all that was good, and bad, about Turner.

When Edward Turner joined Triumph in 1935 as, in his own words "works manager," "sales manager", "general manager" and "chief buyer", the company was seriously short of cash. However, it did have a range of well-designed, and modestly successful, single-cylinder machines, which Turner promptly rebranded with the snappy titles of 'Tiger 70', Tiger '80" and 'Tiger 90 '– the number indicating the bike's supposed top speed.

Admittedly, a 500cc Tiger 90 would only manage a genuine

**1**
**Flo Melling with one of the very first Speed Twins in 1938 – only available to the chosen few!**

**2**
**The Speed Twin was styling perfection. Every rider in 1938 lusted after one.**

90mph on the very best of good days – but there are not many owners of modern Superbikes who have seen a true 187mph from their bikes either! Truly, a case of: "Plus ça change – plus c'est la même chose".

Turner had always been a fan of parallel twins. In fact his Square 4 was actually a pair of conjoined parallel twins. It was no surprise then that when he arrived at Triumph the factory *was* going to have a twin. This was a fortunate set of circumstances because Triumph did, in fact, own an extremely clever, well-designed and attractive twin, which Turner could have immediately utilised. There was however, a five-star problem – at least in Turner's eyes. Triumph's existing twin was a product of the fertile brain of Val Page, who was unquestionably the finest British motorcycle designer of all time - and Turner actively loathed Page.

Therefore, the first job was not to work on the existing twin cylinder engine but, rather, to get rid of Page, who was a genuine genius. With Page bundled off to Ariel, which was also owned by the Sangster family, Turner could get let his ego, and ability, get to work in equal proportions. At this point, just how remarkably perceptive Turner was becomes readily apparent.

"The Speed Twin inculcated the idea in British manufacturers' boardrooms that if you were smart, you could avoid investment in R&D and new models. This mind set was to cost the British dear in the 1960s"

Throughout his working life, Turner was blessed with an uncanny knack of knowing exactly what made motorcyclists buy bikes. This is easy to write but incredibly hard to achieve. Firstly, Turner knew that mass sales would not come from a product that was too great a step from the known and familiar. Innovators are wonderful, but they never make any money. So, Turner's Speed Twin engine looked very much like Triumph's existing twin port single - and many of its competitors, too.

The new engine was actually narrower than the single it replaced, and it was lighter. It was also vastly smoother and made more torque lower down the rev range than its single-cylinder competitors, as well as being easier to start than the singles and much less demanding to ride. In fact, a whole lot of boxes were ticked – and all with minimal financial or technical investment. This sowed the idea that cheap could be good – and later proved fatal to the British bike industry.

With clean external lines and fully enclosed, oil-tight valve gear, the Speed Twin was ultra-modern for 1937 – and was, in every respect, a sophisticated motor. Yet, by having simple push-rod-operated valve gear, the new engine used well-known, and solidly proven, engineering – so development time was minimal.

Turner also made the twin cheap and easy to manufacture so, from day one, the Speed Twin generated profit for Triumph. A key part of the new bike's commercial success was Turner cunningly employed virtually the whole of the Tiger 90 chassis. The new engine simply slotted into the old single's chassis, using nothing more complex than different engine plates.

The four-speed Tiger 90 gearbox was a gem, and the clutch light and efficient. All the single's electrics were well proven so the Speed Twin simply went in to the Tiger 90's bedroom and emptied the cupboards. It was no more complex than that.

Then came the sprinkling of magic dust which Turner, at least at this stage of his career, carried around in his pocket.

He refused to have the steering head angle at the optimum rake for precise handling. To do so would have cramped the lines of the new bike, and Turner wanted it to look lithe, muscular and feline. Finally, he decided on what was to become the world's most famous colour for a motorcycle: Triumph Amaranth Red, set off with hand- painted gold lines on the chromed tank.

This choice was utterly gifted. At a time when black was the standard colour for most of the world's motorcycles, here was a bike which was daring, adventurous and bold, while avoiding being avant-garde, and so discomforting potential buyers. The message was brilliant: 'Buy a Triumph and be different and edgy – but still stay on safe ground'.

The result was a bike so instantly popular that only the most favoured customers were allowed ▸

❶

to buy a Speed Twin from their Triumph dealer: Turner's brand new baby was that desirable!

So, this brings us to the present day and a very interesting situation. On the one hand there are a lot of better 1930s' bikes than a Speed Twin, no matter what criteria are applied – whether it be speed, sophistication or build quality. Critics of the Speed Twin justifiably argue it is the most overrated motorcycle in the world.

Then you see the deep, amaranth red glowing softly in the sun and, truthfully, you would have to loathe bikes not to go weak at the knees. Walk round the Speed Twin, examine it from any angle, lie on the floor even, and try to find a flaw. Even from beneath, the bike is majestically flawless: not merely outstanding but 100%, utterly perfect.

Today, the Speed Twin still holds all the attractions that made it such an instant success in 1938. Gently spin the engine into life and the twin burbles quietly and eagerly. Ease away and the torque is effortless, belying the fact the Speed Twin produced only 27bhp – some third less power than the hot supersports singles of the day.

Cruise at 55-60mph – the sort of speed where the bike would have spent most of its life – and the ride is sublime. Is the Speed Twin something magical? Yes, it is the best.

The handling is also completely in keeping with the bike's performance. Correctly maintained and set up, there is nothing wrong with girder forks and there is a wonderfully anthropomorphic feel in seeing the front end of the bike bob up and down with the road undulations.

This engagement with the rider is enhanced by a touch of pure Turner genius. Rather than having a cluttered area around the top fork yoke, there is just the large friction damper knob and speedometer. All the ancillary gauges are recessed in the petrol tank. This gives a lovely, neat, lithe feel to the bike – even when it is stood still. Truly, Turner did have a feel for what engaged the rider customer.

I much prefer the rigid rear end of the pre-war Speed Twins to the crude, inefficient and heavy sprung hubs of the immediate post-war bikes. In the real world of real classics there is going to be absolutely no problem with a rigid rear end, when the back wheel is wrapped in modern rubber.

The brakes are fine too and provide plenty of practical stopping power for such a light motorcycle so, in every respect, the Speed Twin is one of the most practical pre-war motorcycles you could own.

So that's all the good news. The problem with owning one of these early Speed Twins is they have never been cheap. In the 1970s I was on good terms with Vale-Onslow Motorcycles, and Peter Vale-Onslow, as nice a bike dealer as you could ever wish to meet, had a lovely Speed Twin for sale. Even at a mate's price, it was more expensive than a good motocross bike, and so way outside my budget.

Since then prices have gone up and down, like all commodities, and now they are on the up again. I don't know if sellers are actually getting the £25,000-plus they are asking, but £25k seems to be where good Speed Twins are pitched.

In the cold, objective light of day this is a lot of money for what is quite an ordinary motorcycle in terms of outright speed and handling. Objectively, a four-valve Rudge is a much better option.

Then you stand next to a Speed Twin, with the sun glinting off the chrome on the petrol tank and the amaranth red softly throbbing, and you know, you just absolutely know, that – with the Speed Twin at least – Turner was a genius: there is absolutely no argument about this. And, like all great art, there is a price to pay for perfection.

*Our thanks to Ben Walker of Bonhams for the loan of this bike. Bonhams are the world's leading auctioneers of motorcycles and can be reached on:*
*Ben Walker*
*motorcycles@bonhams.com*
*+44 (0) 8700 273 616.* ◆

**1**
**In truth, the Speed Twin was not a technical masterpiece but it was a wonderful example of production engineering and it works beautifully in practice.**

**2**
**At a time when bikes came in a range of colours including black, black and black, the Speed Twin's Amaranth Red and polished chrome was bold, exciting and highly desirable to anyone with bike blood running through their veins.**

# Egli Fritz

Rarer than a smiling parking
warden with a forgiving nature

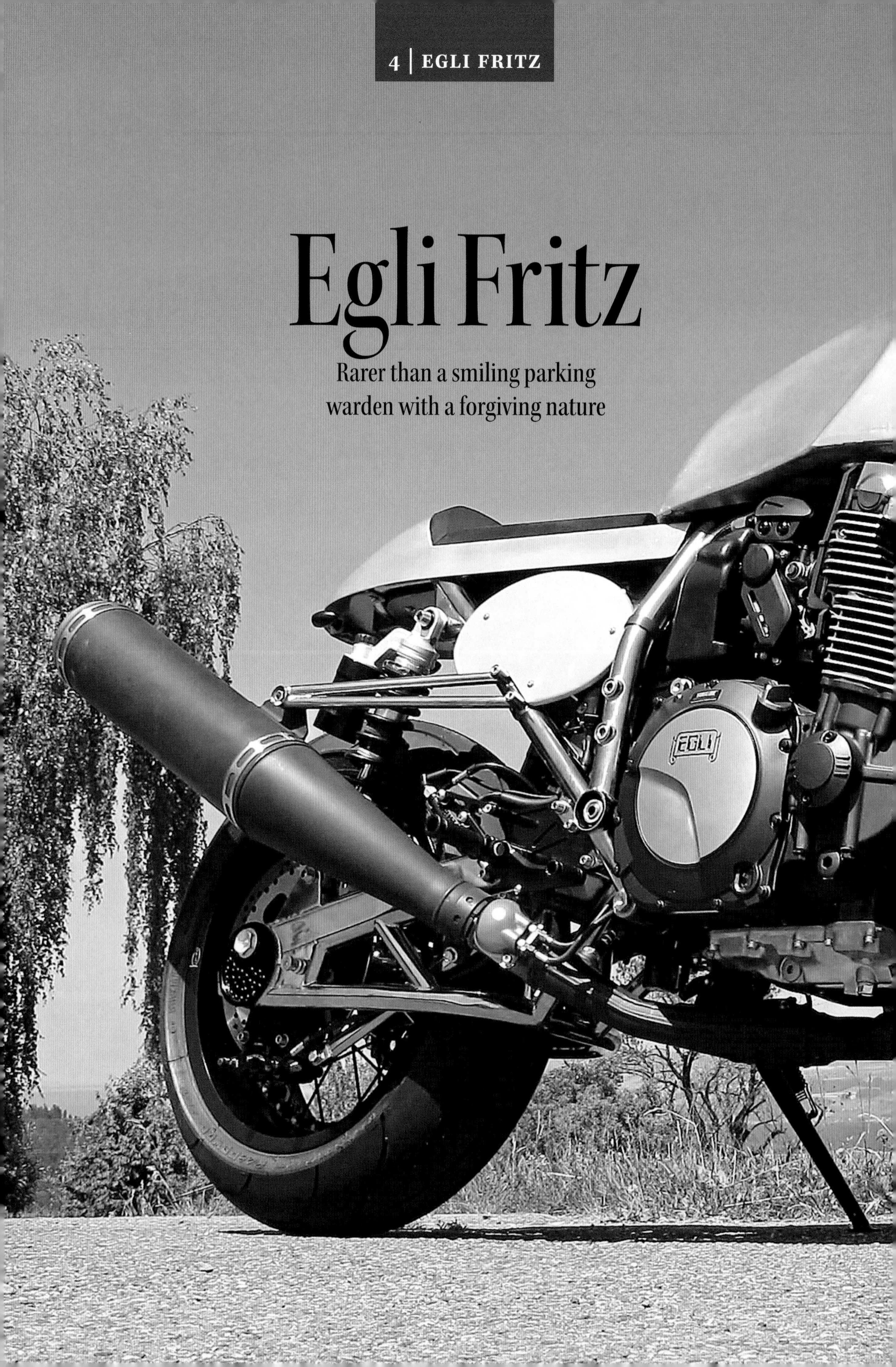

BERINGER
AEROTEC
ÖHLINS
BERINGER

I AM aware that the next few sentences are going to make me sound very, very old – but I want to press on regardless. In ancient times, individual journalists had special relationships with people, or even whole motorcycle factories, and this was both good and bad.

For example, I was the first journalist to see the revolutionary Yamaha power valve on a motocross bike. I was particularly close to some key members of the Yamaha motocross GP team, and I was asked for my opinion of the idea – many months before its existence was known.

There was no need to ask for my discretion because the rules were quite clear: confidential information was private. There was no threat or bribe that could have made me break my word to Yamaha.

I had the same relationship with a number of other manufacturers, including BSA and Triumph.

I was also biased on occasions, and freely admit this. For example, I worshipped Eric Cheney – the British, frame-building genius. Eric was – first, last and middle – flawed goods. He invariably didn't deliver on bikes on time, had a relaxed view as to what constituted a customer deposit, and could be short-tempered.

Against this, we got on very well because he was truly, outstandingly gifted. I called him 'Uncle Eric' and he always

1

2

referred to me as 'Monsieur Melling' because he considered me to be well educated.

And, goodness me, his bikes were brilliant – I still have one today.

My insider position came about because I earned it. I had expert knowledge, worked extremely hard at being a journalist, and could be trusted.

Now, the situation is very different. Trust has in many ways been consigned to the history books. Confidential e-mails are leaked ruthlessly, and with a one-second click of the ubiquitous mobile phone, an image can be ready to distribute throughout the world.

Personally, I want to be able to look at myself in the mirror and see a deeply flawed person, replete with faults, but someone who gives his word and sticks to it. No contracts, non-disclosure payments or any other incentive. Simply giving my promise and keeping to it.

This brings us to the Egli Fritz because I am very biased towards this motorcycle. Viewed with absolute cold objectivity this is not a great motorcycle. But it is a true Classic Superbike and that's why it's here.

The other reason is that I am a huge admirer both of Fritz Egli, the founder of this iconic little company, and of what Alexander Frei and his wife Feli are currently doing with the name.

Finally, in quiet moments between jobs, I look at my copy of The Egli – the Official Book, with its frontispiece signed by Fritz himself together with the message: ***All the best to my friends Carol and Frank, from Fritz Egli***

So to the Egli Fritz – a fabulous, soul-tingling motorcycle with so many faults that it should never have been made.

The Egli story begins with Fritz himself, who raced a ferociously fast Vincent in Swiss hill climbs in the 1960s. He explains. "I was trained as a precision mechanic by AEG and I was taught to an incredibly high standard. I did well and even worked for the company for three years, in Mexico.

"I took this knowledge to motorcycle racing and built a Vincent which was fast but with an engine that was easy to ride. I had a lot of success on the bike but I wanted to move from third places to first, and the handling of the Vincent wouldn't let me do this.

"The problem was that the box-section top frame flexed and there was no fix for this.

"So I would lie awake at night and think of a way to make a bike that would handle and where the frame would be stiff, independently of the engine. This is how the large-diameter spine frame was conceived during the winter of 1966/67.

"I also got rid of the Vincent Girdraulic forks, which were too heavy, and replaced them with forks from the Manx Norton, which were the best available.

"The bike was very successful and I won the Swiss Hill Climb Championship in 1968. Other riders were impressed with my bike and wanted replicas of it and that's how I became a manufacturer."

Egli is housed in a rambling, and deceptively huge, farmhouse right in the centre of the small village of Bettwil, 20 miles south-west of Zurich, in the financial heartland of Switzerland.

Fritz takes up the story again. "I needed somewhere with a lot of space when I started to make motorcycles on a serious commercial level and so we found this derelict place in Bettwil. It was so bad that you could stand in the basement and see the sky right through every floor, all the way to the roof. That's a building in really bad condition!

"But, with the help of a lot of friends, we eventually restored it and there is a lot of room – which is what we wanted in 1970."

After the legendary Egli Vincent, Fritz went on to produce a remarkable range of bikes, mainly with Japanese engines ▸

**1**
**The Fritz is surprisingly slim for an across the frame four cylinder motorcycle.**

**2**
**One day Melling will grow up and become sensible - or maybe not.**

but occasionally a Ducati, too. Eventually, the strain of looking after 12 full-time employees became too much and Fritz let it be known the business could be bought: and that's when the trouble started.

"I had so many dreamers come to see me – people who were in love with the Egli legend but had no idea of the reality of running a business making motorcycles. They wanted to sit in the office all day, playing on computers or chatting on the phone, and they didn't realise that Egli was hard work.

"There is no going home at 5 o'clock and locking the door. Sometimes, you work for 12 hours without a break. Sometimes you work longer, and you get your hands dirty, too. That's the reality of manufacturing.

"Then Alex came along and he was serious - and so I was happy to let the Egli name go to him."

'Alex' is Alexander Frei, a successful entrepreneur with a family business based around water treatment technology. As well as knowing how to run a business, Alex was a successful car racer and was the 2004 Le Mans Endurance Champion, so he understands exactly the passion that has been behind Egli for all these years.

Alex was a fan of Egli Vincents when he was a teenager but could never afford one. Initially, he didn't even know that Egli was for sale but once he found out it took only six months to conclude the deal. The hardest part was analysing the business case because Egli isn't a hobby for Alex. He was attracted by the idea of reviving the Egli brand and relaunching the Egli Motorcycle Manufacturing Company in Switzerland.

The Egli Fritz is the first manifestation of this dream. The idea was to make a traditional Egli, characterised by the huge central spine, but with a modern engine and running gear.

The design process took a year and a half, and things became somewhat rushed in order to get the first run of six machines completed before the end of 2016, and so just scrape in under the more relaxed Euro 3 emission regulations.

Egli says the aim was to build, "...a typical café racer but with modern geometry true to the Egli slogan of 'rides as if on rails'."

The bike's geometry is based around a steering head rake of 24.5°, which is true sports territory. For example, a Ducati Panigale is only 0.5° steeper. Yamaha's XSR 900 Abarth, as pure a café racer as you are going to get from a Japanese manufacturer, is right in the same area as the Fritz, with 25° of rake and a 1440mm wheelbase. Don't expect to go for a cruise in the countryside, Honda CB1100 style, on the Fritz.

Attached to the archetypal Egli frame is Öhlin's suspension, front and back, and – as one would expect – this is excellent. Equally impressive are the twin 297mm, six-piston front brakes. I like powerful front brakes. Even this is not true. I actually love powerful anchors, and braking is the only thing I could legitimately claim to do really well when racing but...

The big but is that these brakes are inordinately fierce and will lock the front wheel in a blink. Racing on grippy tarmac, with a total absence of farm tractors, half asleep pedestrians and distracted people pushing prams out into the road, these would be dream brakes but, goodness me, Egli Fritz owners need to be very circumspect in terms of grabbing a handful of front brake lever in anything other than perfect conditions. For me, my middle finger, gently applied, was all the force I needed to scrub off speed in race time.

Getting rid of the standard Yamaha running gear and substituting it with bespoke Egli parts sheds a whopping 36kgs – 80lbs in real money.

The power for the Fritz comes from Yamaha's very traditional 1251cc inline four, which was normally found in the XJR 1300. This DOHC motor was born in 1984, living in the FJ1100, and has now been phased out of Yamaha's offering. In the past, I quite liked the five-speed air-/oil-cooled engine, but now it feels decidedly old fashioned – unfortunately, not in the sense of harking back to something better but rather simply not as good as other power plants being currently offered by retro manufacturers.

Even with these caveats, the engine is okay. Egli run it in bog-standard form, and there's nothing wrong with this. There's a stonking amount of torque available at almost

**1**
**Or you could be riding a sensible, fuel efficient scooter wearing a high vis vest.**

**2**
**Tiny keyless entry.**

**3**
**Ultra minimalist information centre is very much an acquired taste.**

**1**

any rpm and the 100 or so horses galloping away inside the Yamaha's crankcases will ensure you can lose your licence in a blink, so there's no problem there. It's simply a case of not being an engine you dream about having in a retro bike.

Not that Yamaha went out of their way to support the Egli Fritz project. If you want a brand new XJR1300 chassis, Egli has a row of them in the basement – complete in every detail except for the engine!

So now we come to the things that make this motorcycle very, very special. The Egli chassis, Öhlins' suspension, and even the underwear soiling front brake are all magnificent: truly awe-inspiring.

The Kineo wire wheels, cunningly permitting the use of tubeless tyres, are great too, but then things go downhill and, even as an Egli fan, you just have to start questioning what the heck were they thinking about.

The single instrument binnacle contains, allegedly, a speedometer and some other bits of information, but was so utterly illegible that it was worthless. The multiple tiny buttons, for stopping the engine and operating the indicators were also a disaster.

There is a silly, keyless entry system, too. I like keyless entry on cars. A big button that unlocks doors, opens the rear tail gate and starts the car is good and practical. But the Egli system, sourced from Motogadget, along with the switches, is just an affectation in the form of a tiny circle of metal, which can't be attached to a key ring and doesn't switch off the engine either.

All these custom bike pretensions are fine for a show machine, which has an exhaust pipe made from chocolate and a saddle covered with ant skins, but is the Fritz a custom bike – or is it, in the tradition of Eglis over the years, a thoroughly practical motorcycle?

The truth turned out to be that the Fritz was a rather a good, hard-core café racer. I'm not really interested in hearing people moan about clip ons and rear set footrests. What do you expect on a Caff – cruise control and a stereo? Go buy a Gold Wing if you do.

For me, the riding position wasn't sufficiently radical. There was ample enough room to make the 'bars lower and shorter so you could become authentically crippled by trying to ride a race bike on the road.

What I couldn't come to terms with was the saddle height of the bike. I am 5ft 11in and even for me, it was a stretch to get both feet on the floor. Part of the problem was that on the test bike, which was Alex's own machine, the alloy fuel tank and seat pan were from the first experimental machine.

On production bikes, if six machines can be considered to be a run, the seat unit is curved and this makes the floor an easier reach. Even so, have a look at the static images of the bike and you'll see there is an awful lot of space between the bottom of the exhaust and the solid ground beneath.

So there I am, being a typical nit-picking journalist, which is fair enough until the Fritz is tipped into a corner at 70mph and suddenly all is forgiven. The motorcycle really does handle beautifully and the speed is scrubbed off so effortlessly that you want all motorcycles to have this suicidally powerful braking available.

Best of all for me was that, on the apex of a corner ▸

**4**
**1250cc Yamaha XJR engine is authentically classic.**

"The Fritz's handling was pure Egli – drum tight and laser accurate."

where we were shooting pictures, there was an example of Switzerland's best road repairs with a strip of zero grip tarmac. On every pass, the Fritz wriggled about and then came completely back on to line with no input from me – very impressive, and a great credit to the engineering behind the bike.

Now, here's where things get slightly complex. The six examples of the Fritz were sold instantly on launch and no-one blinked over the £42,000 price – not for a nano second. And, in some respects, the Fritz is a complete bargain for the wealthy who are seeking exclusivity.

The problem, if it is an issue at all, is there are much better café racer/retros about for vastly less money. The 'go to' choice has to be Triumph's Thruxton R, and this will set you back around £14,000, depending on the level of bling.

Even more affordable is the new Kawasaki Z900RS, which is around £12,000 – again bling dependent.

Now – I know both of these are common-or-garden production bikes and the Fritz is a hand-built special but, even so, £30,000 or so is a mammoth gulf – especially when the Egli still looks like a work in progress.

I admire everything Alex and his team are doing with Egli, and spending an hour with Fritz Egli himself was a real privilege. I look forward to the next project from Bettwil and one which is perhaps a more finished product while still retaining the Egli DNA. ◆

**1**
**A seriously impressive Retro**

**2**
**Fritz Egli.**

**3**
**Minimalist front end is very custom bike and is an acquired taste.**

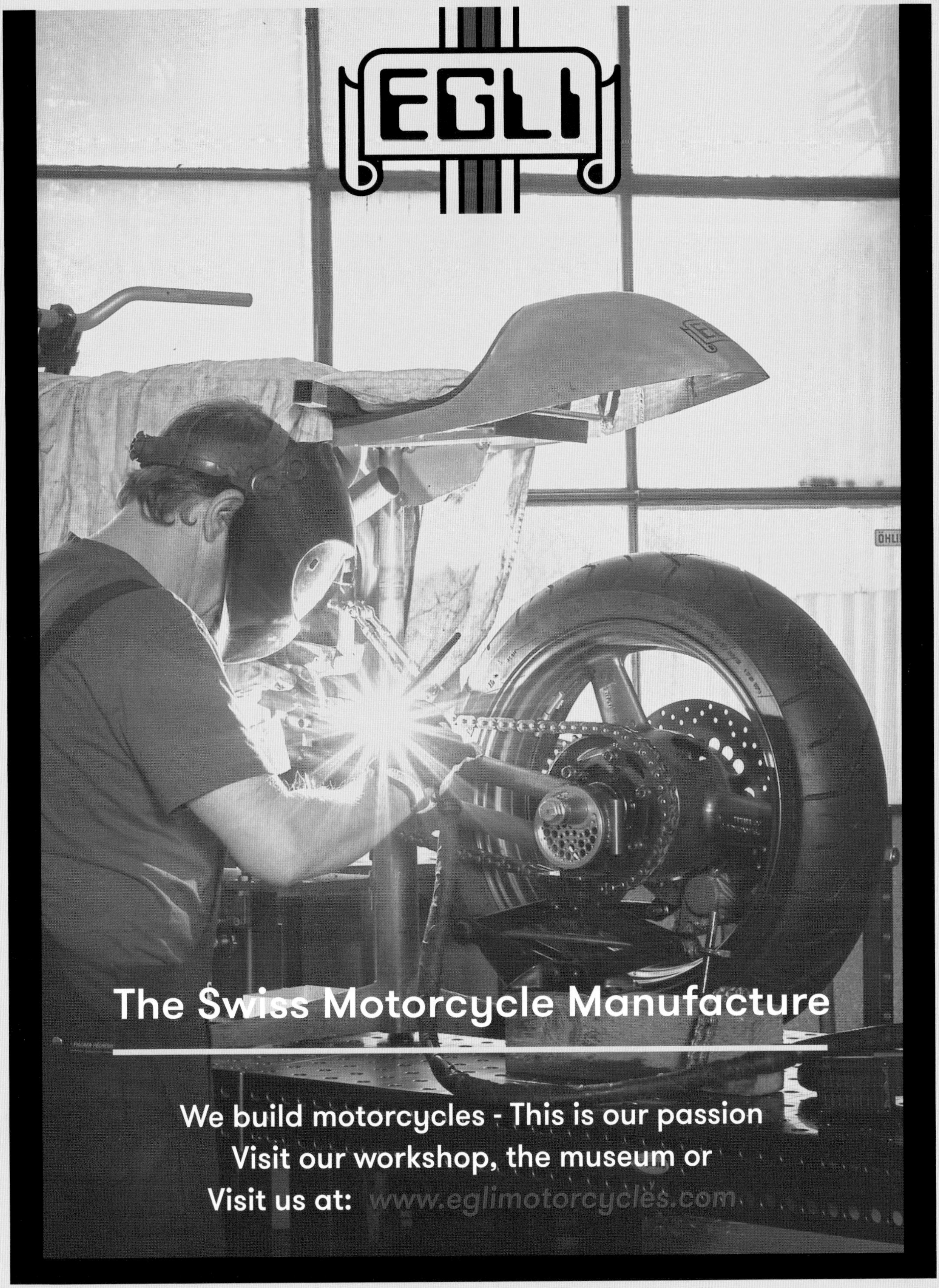
EGLI
The Swiss Motorcycle Manufacture
We build motorcycles - This is our passion
Visit our workshop, the museum or
Visit us at: www.eglimotorcycles.com

Arai
Weise
DUCATI

# Ducati 900SS

## Dreams are made of this

WINSTON Churchill's famous quote: "History is written by the victors…" was never more applicable than with the Ducati 900SS.

At its launch in 1974, Ducati was staggering on the point of extinction, with most of the Borgo Panigale factory being used to make diesel engines for Alfa Romeo. Almost as an after-thought, Ducati motorcycles trickled out in fits and starts and were of truly, breathtakingly poor quality.

At the time, no-one with a grain of brain would go near a 900SS. Ducati loyalists get very tense when this is said, but the truth is the best superbike of the day was the Kawasaki Z1 – which not only out accelerated the 900SS but had a higher top speed, a beautiful finish and whose maintenance was confined to regular oil changes and washing the bike once a week. None of these traits applied to the SS.

If you didn't fancy a Z1, and everyone with a decent dose of testosterone in their veins did, then Suzuki offered you the fast, stone-axe reliable and sweet-handling GS 750.

In fact, the situation was quite dire in terms of what the SS did offer the rider.

There were two problems.

The first was the rather quirky nature of the bike itself. There is no doubt certain parts of the SS are genius and this is why criticising the bike evokes harsh reactions from Ducati fans. Ing. Fabio Taglioni's v-twin engine is a thing of mechanical beauty and, even in the depths of Ducati's worst moments, the engines were well made. Much of this quality is down to Taglioni's hand being heavily on what bits of the production process he could control. The problem was much of the bike was out of his hands.

So, let's go back to the very roots of the SS because it's an interesting story – and the US Army Air Force has an important part to play in it.

Before the Second World War, Ducati was a radio company – and an extremely successful one. Motorcycles were not on the agenda in any shape, way or form.

The Ducati brothers, Bruno and Cavalieri, were world leaders in the production of short-wave radios and, since 1924, had been the key supplier to the Italian navy. This was a good thing in that it made the Ducati brothers a lot of money and, in 1935, they were able to open a state-of-the-art factory at Borgo Panigale, in Bologna, employing more than 7,000 staff.

The factory was air-conditioned and used the very latest, and the very best, machine tools available in the world to manufacture precision components. That was the good news.

The bad news for the brothers was the Ducati factory became a 'must-bomb' attraction for Allied Air Forces during the Italian campaign. The American 15th Air Force was particularly determined to take out Ducati – and achieved its aim with great success, totally razing the factory to the ground. Having a large, smoking hole where your factory used to be was not immediately helpful to Ducati.

But the good news was to follow after the war ended. Because of Ducati's high-tech reputation pre-war, the Italian government re-equipped and modernised the factory with, this time, state of the art, 1950s machine tools. This actually put Ducati in a stronger position than other Italian factories in the north of the country which weren't bombed.

Thus, a fortunate turn of fate provided Ducati with an ace card to play. Uniquely among all the European manufacturers, the Bologna factory was capable of mass- producing a complex engine. This was the single most important factor in the evolution of the sophisticated, overhead cam, desmodromic engines.

Ducati was about to be given another ace card. In 1954, the company was staggering on the very edge of bankruptcy being effectively Government-owned and kept barely alive with subsidies. In fact, even paying the few workers employed in making motorcycles was proving very difficult. Ducati's rival Mondial had just won the prestigious Moto Giro d'Italia, but the young designer who played such a large part in the success was not invited to the post-race party. The designer

was Fabio Taglioni, and this is how he remembers the incident:

"I arrived at the racing department of Mondial, owned by the Boselli brothers, and was hired immediately.

"That year the federation came up with the Tour of Italy. We were inexperienced. In fact, though we won each leg, we lost the Tour overall. In the second year, we won. But I was not invited to the victory celebration dinner.

"The following day, I left – without giving an explanation.

"It was then I received a proposal which was destined to change my life forever. I was called in by the general manager of Ducati Meccanica, who was Mr Montano, a man of sterling character, a great company manager, who said, and I quote: 'I know your talent and I need you. If you build 100 motorcycles to win the Tour of Italy, Ducati will stay open, because I only have one month's salary for my workers. If not, we shut down and everyone goes home'."

In the 1950s, events like the Milano-Taranto and Moto Giro D'Italia, which were held on public roads, were more important to motorcycle sales in Italy than Grand Prix racing or even winning the Isle of Man TT. These Italian races were long-distance trials of speed and endurance and success meant instant sales.

Taglioni designed a bevel drive, sohc engine which appeared simultaneously in 100cc and 125cc forms to give Ducati two chances in the multi-class Moto Giro. The bike ▸

bore many of Taglioni's trademark design traits, and like all his work, it was a very conservative concept breaking no new ground. On the contrary, Taglioni's trademark was thorough, sound designs which worked in mass production.

Norton, in particular, had been racing bevel drive engines since the 1920s with incredible success. Unit construction engines, where the engine and gearbox are one item, had also been in production since before the First World War. What Taglioni did was to put all the best-known engineering practices into one, unified package. The result was a neat, reliable and very beautiful motorcycle.

Almost simultaneously, there was a series of disasters in road racing events throughout Europe. In 1955, 82 spectators were killed in a single accident when a Mercedes car somersaulted over the pit wall at Le Mans, and the accidents were piling up in the Moto Giro and Milano-Taranto, too. In 1957 the original Moto Giro ended.

Despite the demise of the Moto Giro, Ducati were still left with an extremely marketable, race-inspired road bike – the truly magnificent 175 Sport. The Sport, launched at the Milan Show in November 1956, incorporated all the lessons and characteristics of race bikes in a hot, road bike package.

The engine was a typical Taglioni design. The heart of the Sport was an over square – 62mm x 57.8mm – high-revving, single overhead camshaft motor. As with all Taglioni's engines, the cam was driven by a shaft, and the wet sump kept the oil low in the chassis. The engine was simple but still needing precision tooling to manufacture. In standard trim, power was a class leading 14bhp at an astonishing 8,000rpm. This gave an 85mph plus performance – comparable with many 500s of its day.

The road bike's racing brother carried the exotic name Silverstone Super. For this machine Ducati provided a hotter cam, bigger carburettor, race exhaust and rev counter. A small pilot, glued to the fuel tank and with his knees tucked in, could expect to see a genuine 95mph – which was Grand Prix performance.

The next big step forward for Ducati was when Taglioni produced the iconic 'L' configuration v-twin. This remarkable engine took much of the well-proven technology from the singles and combined it with a light, slim and powerful 750cc engine.

Justification for Taglioni's new machine came at the 1972 Imola 200 race when Paul Smart beat the best Superbikes of the day to give Ducati a legendary victory. How much this success was against the run of play can be judged by the fact no-one else except Smart, who needed to put food on the family table, would take the Ducati ride.

Sadly, Ducati lacked the resources to exploit the publicity bonanza which followed, and the normal pattern of staggering along the edge of financial crisis continued unabated.

Taglioni continued to make the best of his scant resources and, in 1974, the 750 was stretched to 864cc, and now there was a claimed 70hp available – but only for the lucky owner who got a good engine.

'Ducatisti' will tell you that the very best of all the 900s is the 1975 model, which had the right-hand gear change for which the motor was designed, and was unconstrained by noise or emission controls.

So what did you get in 1975? First, there was Taglioni's unique, and crack cocaine addictive, 90° v-twin – complete with desmodromic valve gear.

**Ridden hard, on fast curves, the bike gave a magic carpet ride'**

"Fire up the motor and you will be greeted with a magnificent cacophony of clanks and whirrs from the engine - and the booming braaahhh, braaahhh, braaahhh from the barely restrained Conti silencers. You could easily overdose on mechanical ecstasy.."

**1**
**Mike Hailwood at Ballaugh Bridge, making his epic TT win look easy.**

**2**
**The ancillary bits of the MH900 were very utilitarian.**

**3**
**Big V Twin is unmistakably Ducati.**

No matter what anyone thinks about any other part of the 900SS there are few more beautiful engines in the world than these Ducati air-cooled twins, and even fewer more anthropomorphic. Kick the motor into life, and you will be greeted with a magnificent cacophony of clanks and whirrs from the engine and the booming braaahhhh, braaahhhh from the barely restrained Conti silencers. You could easily overdose on mechanical ecstasy!

The engine works okay, too. It's not Z1 quick but it is deceptively brisk and lopes along like a wolf on the scent. The clutch, if well maintained, is fine and the gearbox works, too.

The cockpit is immense. For some reason, Taglioni insisted on having a mammoth 59in wheelbase. This means the 900SS has more space than a GP star's motorhome. The result is ultra-stable handling, particularly on fast bends, but also a bike which needs muscling about. This is not a motorcycle that you are going to flick through tight bends.

The Marzocchi front forks are fine for the period and the twin Brembo discs are excellent – better than the Japanese offerings of the day.

All this was the good news. The bad news filled every other space. First, the build quality was appalling. A good SS fairing looks as if it was done between screwing diesel engines together – and a bad one is really dreadful.

The frames are all over the place, ranging in quality from good to appalling, while the electrics are consistently bad. Compared with the Japanese opposition, only the truly dedicated loved the SS.

For all these reasons, the SS sold poorly, and finding a retail customer in the vital American market was the nearest thing to impossible the motorcycling world could offer.

What Ducati needed was a huge marketing coup which would give world-wide publicity – but one that cost nothing because the factory was, quite literally, penniless.

Let's re-cap. The 900SS had less power than the Japanese bikes, a wheelbase that was unsuitable for most race tracks and no support to offer to teams. How could this be turned into a success story?

The answer was two-fold. By a complete quirk of fate, the 900SS was perfect for the Isle of Man TT and its 37¾ miles of high-speed public roads. What better place could you put an ultra-stable, torquey race bike?

The problem was the TT was nearly in as bad a way as Ducati. It was no longer a Grand Prix race, and factory support was long past the golden days of screaming Hondas and wailing MVs.

Then the planets moved into alignment and the sun appeared. Out of retirement came a bald, 38-year-old, slightly inarticulate, PR averse and achingly modest Moto God. It was Mike Hailwood – still the greatest motorcycle racer in many observers' eyes.

It was the stuff of legends and, like the best Hollywood blockbusters, the hero triumphed, as Hailwood won – and on a Ducati 900SS.

Following his win, the world, and not just the bike press, went into Hailwood mania, and so Ducati was persuaded to off-load a few of its stockpile of unsold V-Twins by giving them a quick, and it really was quick, paint job – replicating Hailwood's race winning 900SS – and a road-legal steel fuel tank.

The first, and in Ducati's eyes the only, production run was of 200 bikes, and I was told by a Ducati insider the view was ▸

since Coburn and Hughes, then the British Ducati importer, was jumping up and down demanding a Hailwood replica they might as well invest a few lira in a cheap paint job and have the bikes sat unsold in Britain, rather than having them collect cobwebs in a corner of a diesel engine factory.

It was one of the great marketing mistakes of all time – but one which Ducati soon corrected!

The first 200 Hailwood replicas were sold before the paint was dry, and then Ducati swung into full action converting virtually all of the 900s into Hailwood replicas.

Eventually, Ducati made something in the region of 7,000 Hailwood replicas and probably the same number of 900s have been converted privately. In our area of England, I know of one motorcycling paint shop that had an almost full-time production line transforming standard 900s into Hailwood replicas – things became that frenetic.

I was lucky enough to ride a genuine Hailwood Ducati. It was a truly memorable experience and one which evoked a lot of different reactions.

Firstly, the Ducati really does look something like Hailwood rode, which isn't surprising because the race bike was so closely related to its road going sibling. For sure, it is big enough – stretching out in every direction with enough room to house a couple of modern superbikes inside the vast fairing. Then my eyes fall on the appalling paint work, the welds that look as if they'd been done by someone on their third bottle of bad Chianti, and ancillary equipment that redefines mediocrity. Surely, such an iconic motorcycle can't be that bad?

But then there is the engine. Ing. Taglioni's magnificent bevel drive Desmo twin sits imperiously like an aristocrat in a tenement block. The alloy gleams softly, the cylinder heads curve sensuously and the exhausts flow anthropomorphically like rock pythons at rest. Is this the most beautiful engine to grace a production motorcycle?

Dave Brown, the MH900's owner, cracks up the big Desmo Twin – and the dreadful paintwork and the battery held in place with a rubber strap are instantly forgotten. The 864cc Twin sounds like a pair of Manx Nortons and produces pure overhead camshaft racing music – clanking valve gear, accompanied by a powerful boom from the twin Conti silencers.

Not standard, but possibly the best aftermarket product made, are the transparent Perspex covers at the cylinder head end of the bevel drive. A product of 'Doctor Desmo', these allow the rider to observe the valve gear in all its mechanical glory while necessarily suppressing any thoughts of the cost if a tooth came off one of the bevel drive gears.

One does not so much ride on the MH Ducati but rather in it. Compared with even a classic GP race bike, like a Matchless G.50, the MH's cockpit is huge. Against its contemporary race bred rivals, such as a Rob North Triumph/BSA Triple, it's even bigger. However, standing alongside the monsters of the late-1970s machines produced by the Japanese, the Hailwood bike really starts to seem quite svelte.

Gear selection requires a firm action, but the pinions engage without a problem and then we're off. The sun is beating down on the Anglesey Race Circuit – which is only 60 miles across the Irish Sea from the Isle of Man – and it is difficult not to feel the spirit of Hailwood riding with me, as the big Desmo gobbles up the sweeping curves and descents of one of Europe's best race circuits.

Intellectually, I know Dave's Hailwood replica is just that: a 900SS with a paint job. But the booming Twin pounding away beneath me, the vibration running through my hands and the ultra-steady handling brought about by the 59-in wheelbase, make it easy to suspend reality for half an hour.

Hailwood revved the Sports Motorcycles' bike to 8,500rpm at peak – although this was getting towards the fragile end of reliability for the Desmo engine. The rev limit for a standard road bike is 7,000rpm, but I change at 6,500rpm for fear of missing a gear and something horrendously expensive happening. With all unrestored bikes one has to be conscious of the fact all those bits whirling around are not as young as they once were – and they need to be treated with respect.

My self-imposed rev limit is not a problem because, despite breathing through a pair of huge 40mm Dell'Orto carbs, the Desmo is perfectly civilised and has none of the coughing or hesitation of a Manx Norton or G.50 before the motor comes on the cam. If you wanted a motor apparently designed for the TT, this would be it.

The handling too would have been TT perfect. The space

**1**
**The MH 900 is very close, spiritually at least, to Hailwood's race bike – although still a standard 900SS under the skin.**

**2**
**Ducati were quick to latch onto the golden ticket which Hailwood's win gave them.**

"A long, sweeping, uphill bend with the v-twin engine pulling hard and the twin Contis snarling. Motorcycling does not come any better."

1

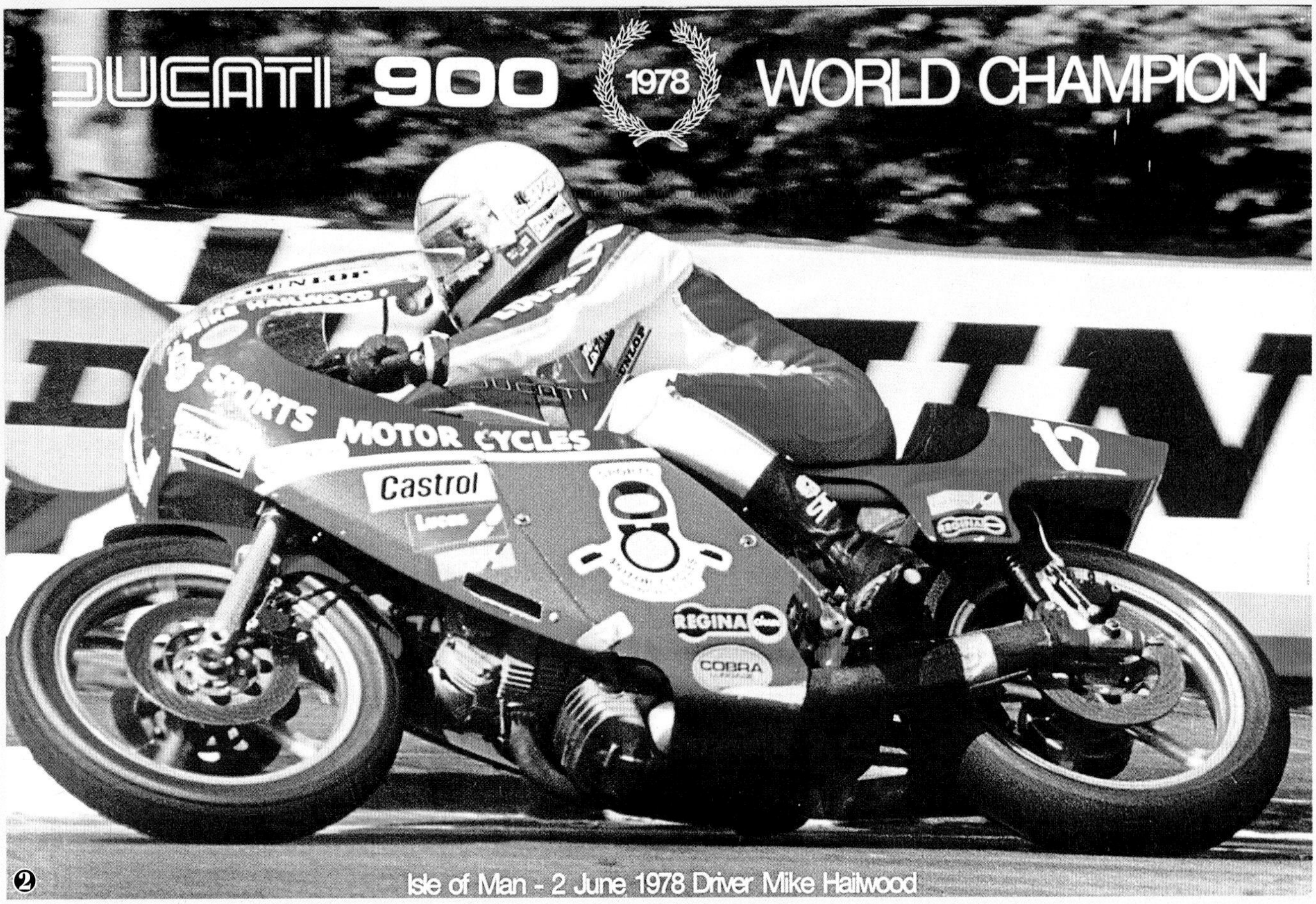


inside the cockpit makes for a Rolls-Royce ride and the 4.76-gallon tank is wonderfully supportive. Get your head down behind the fairing and this bike will really romp along.

No doubt the Marzocchi suspension would get frazzled when pushed hard – as it did originally – but I am riding this very valuable motorcycle with a lot of circumspection.

Of course, there is a problem on the tight sections of the track. This is a motorcycle that really demands physical input for quick changes of direction. That wonderful stability which makes the Ducati such a dream on fast curves becomes a nuisance when the bike has to be pushed into tight corners.

Tucking down over the 4.76-gallon tank on a long straight, it's easy to see how Hailwood accomplished such impressive speeds in the TT.

It's not so much that the bike won't stop or turn – the twin 280mm Brembo discs are surprisingly effective – but rather it would prefer not to be pushed around and makes its feelings known.

But then we're back on to the long, curving right-hand straight at Anglesey and the speed just builds up relentlessly. The road bike gives 70hp: Hailwood's machine had another 17hp on top of that and he was much lighter. Suddenly, the 175mph that Mike's bike managed in the TT, seems highly credible.

As I pull the Ducati onto its centre-stand I have answered my own questions. Is the riding experience worth the appalling paint, dangling electric cables and crude finish? Without a doubt!

I'm going to get saving now. ◆

Our thanks to arch Ducati enthusiast Dave Brown for the loan of his MH900.

Thanks also to the fabulous Anglesey Circuit, for providing the best place in the world to try the bike.

DUNLOP
MIKE HAILWOOD
COBRA
SPORTS
MOTOR CYCLES
12
CHAMPION
N.C.R.
Castrol
CHAMPION

# The 1978 Formula One TT

The day I shed two tiny tears watching a race...

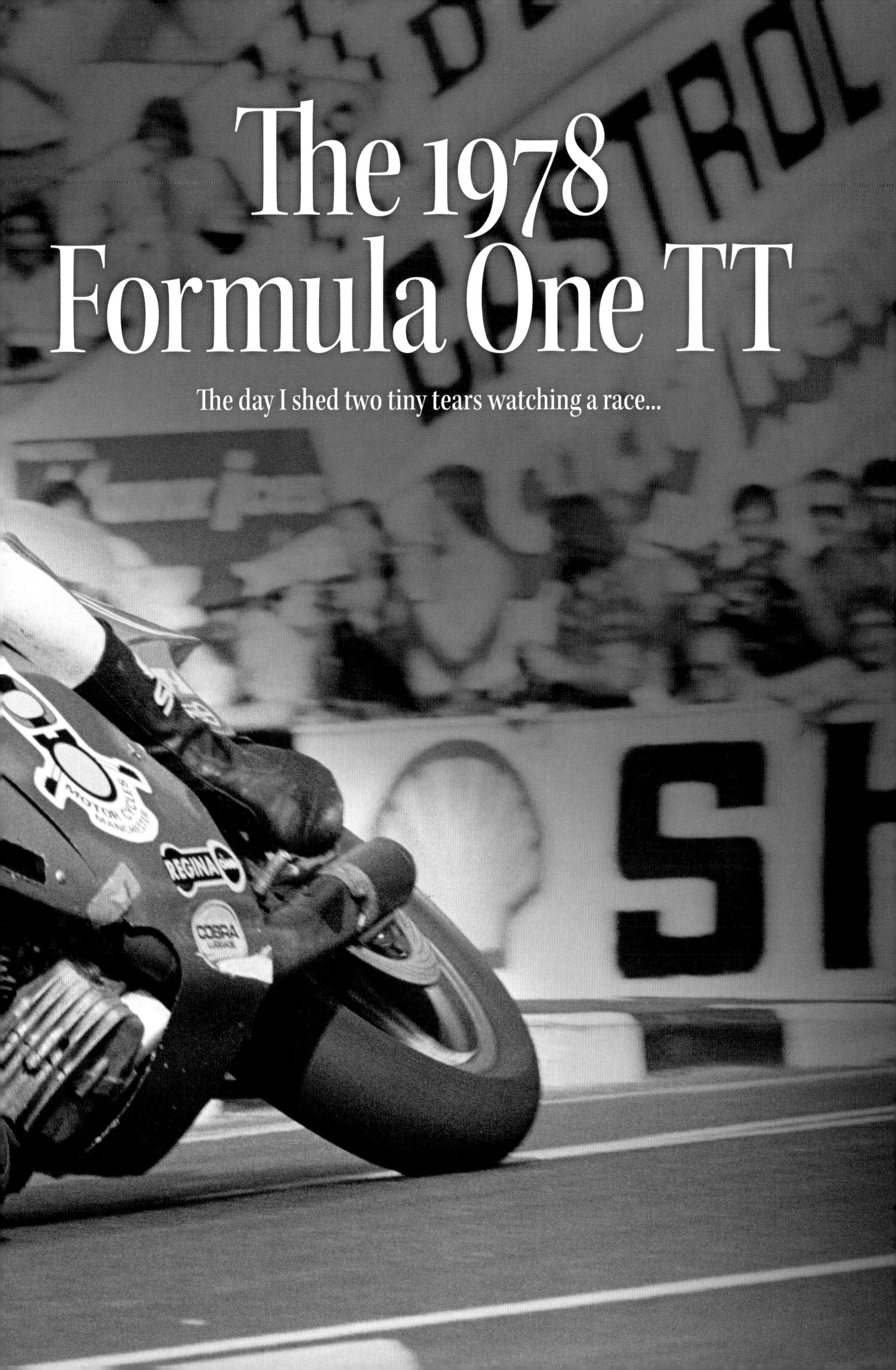

I wrote this chapter in the depths of a miserable British winter with the rain lashing down and temperatures hovering just above freezing – but merely thinking about the immortal Mike Hailwood has lifted my spirits.

There will always be arguments regarding who is the greatest racing motorcyclist of all time and, in many ways, the question is irrelevant because every era is so much different from the one which went before it.

To my mind, Valentino Rossi is probably the greatest because of the sheer range of his ability in terms not only of racing but also his ruthless marketing skills and team leadership.

But Rossi is not a rider to whom I can warm. Businessman, media star, MotoGod – but never one of us, the club racers who pay our entry fees and ride our bikes for the sheer love of the sport.

By contrast, Mike Hailwood was a true racing deity – while still being so incredibly ordinary. Hailwood was disorganised like us; Hailwood treated racing as a hobby just like us; and Hailwood was vastly more interested in riding bikes than in developing them.

Where he differed was his prodigious talent. 'Mike the Bike' could win on any bike, of any type and of any capacity – and beat any rider in the world in the process. Just imagine a rider who would race a four-cylinder, four-stroke machine and a two-stroke twin in the same day – and be on the podium in both races.

Hailwood needed no practice, no machine set-up and no experience of the machine he was riding. He simply got on anything with two wheels and won.

He was also modest, kind, generous and incredibly brave. In fact, for us club racers, scratching around in the mud at the bottom of the motorcycle racing pond, he was our hero.

1978 was also a seminal moment in my life because I was beginning to become a grown up – or at least as adult as I was ever going to be. In the previous autumn I had been promoted to head of department–and at an extremely young age, too.

"At this point, it is important to realise just how delightfully amateurish the Sports Motorcycles' effort was in some ways."

Now I had management responsibilities in addition to my normal work, and these were growing by the day.

In addition to my full-time "day" job, I was also writing for magazines all over the world as well as racing enduros at international level.

When I hinted that I wanted time off to go the TT my boss told me, and bluntly too, that I needed to decide what I wanted to do with my life.

In fact, the decision was quite easy. I was enjoying the responsibilities I now had, every bit as much as racing or writing, and wanted to progress even further. It wasn't just the money, which was important, but more the thrill of seeing my ideas come to fruition.

For me, planning wasn't something to be tolerated and executed with the minimum of time and effort – but a real pleasure. I absolutely loved working things out, writing proposals and then watching as the ideas unfolded.

So, for all these reasons seeing the Hailwood comeback was out of the question. But…

The enormous, galactic-sized "but" was that this was Hailwood – probably the only real hero I have had in my entire life. Mike wasn't merely admired, he was worshipped, and so not seeing him ride in the TT would have been a crime for which I would never have forgiven myself.

The problem was how to see Hailwood race and be back at work, bright and keen, on Monday morning.

The solution came through the friend of a friend of a friend. He knew an ex-RAF pilot who would fly me, with my then wife and her friend too, to the Isle of Man very early on the Saturday of race week – and Saturday was the day of the Formula One race in which Hailwood was riding the Ducati. He would then get us back late on Saturday and I could be at my desk on Monday completely untarnished.

It was a cash only job–and no receipts.

We duly arrived at the General Aviation side of Liverpool Airport and the pilot told us that the job was off. There was a thick mist and the little plane he had borrowed was just not up to flying in these conditions.

Away from my wife, I took him on one side for a chat. I had been told he had flown Hawker Hunter fighter bombers during the civil war in Oman and was an authentically determined pilot – a proper hard case! Now I needed some commitment.

First, I explained the significance of the flight. I wasn't going to watch a motorcycle race – I was going to see Hailwood. Short of having a personal interview with God, things couldn't be more important.

Then I offered him an extra £20. This doesn't sound much now but I guess it's about the current equivalent of £125 – and a lot more money than I could sensibly, or even stupidly, afford.

Health and Safety was vastly more relaxed than it is today and monitoring of flights was very loose too. So we loaded up, with me in the right-hand seat – quietly hoping I didn't get a close up view of the Irish Sea as we hit it.

The little Cessna bumped down the runway and, after what seemed like several years, we clawed our way through the mist and cloud and into a bright blue sky. There had been no conversation…

Now, the issue was that we were behind schedule. Over the headphones, I stressed the need to be there on time – and slid him another tenner. Whatever was in that flat-four, Lycoming engine, he found it!

By now, our pilot had really bought into the whole trip. He radioed a mate he had at Ronaldsway, the Isle of Man's airport, and asked him to have a suitably, sportingly minded taxi driver ready to meet us when we landed.

And they were as good as their word. As the little Cessna taxied to a halt on the General Aviation side of Ronaldsway, there was the taxi, with its engine running, just a few yards away. Now, we had to get to Glen Helen, one of my favourite viewing spots on the TT course, before the roads closed.

It's not only TT racers who are quick on public roads – Manx taxi drivers can be, too!

We piled into the bashed up little black Peugeot – and the metaphorical flag dropped.

I did remember to wish the fairies good luck as we hurtled down to their bridge at Malew, but not for me. I wanted all the good fortune to go to Mike.

Our chauffeur hurled the Peugeot like a rally car and I was all smiles. By contrast, there was a deafening silence from the two passengers in the back seat.

We arrived in ample time, well, just about enough time, to get a space high above the circuit on the apex of the climbing left-hand bend which is Glen Helen.

I have to confess that, almost always, I am a poor spectator. Invariably, I want to do whatever I am watching rather than just observe it. But this was different and I need to convey just how much Hailwood meant to us ordinary folk – not the great and the good and the famous, but the common people, who are the heart and life of motorcycling.

Every time Hailwood appeared, the crowd cheered and clapped. I am sure there were supporters of other riders, but they were swallowed by the immense waves of emotion that were defining this epic moment. ▸

DUNLOP
CASTROL
Cycle News
CHAMPION
12

On every lap, Hailwood touched down the fairing in precisely the same place on the bend and, on every lap, a gasp went up which seemed to shake the trees.

We rode the bike with Hailwood and were part of his win in a way no other rider, current or in the past, could inculcate. It was a magical moment and unique in my whole motorcycling life.

I was desperate to go to the paddock but what very few molecules of common sense that I possessed, and they were very few, prevailed. The taxi driver took us back to Ronaldsway at a suitably sedate pace and we cruised back to Liverpool in the Cessna, at a relaxed 140mph.

On the return journey, my wife and her friend were quite chatty, but I was almost silent. I was aware, even hours after the race, that I had seen something special – a legend creating a legend – and turning fantasy into fact.

Thank you Mike.

Many years later, I worked with Steve Wynne, the genius behind Hailwood's win. This is the story behind the race, told by the person at the very centre of the story. Steve tells a wonderful tale not only of one marvellous day in June but also gives a great insight into Hailwood's character – and his unique talents.

In the mid-1970s, Steve owned Sports Motorcycles in Manchester. It was an idea way ahead of its time, with a large, well-lit showroom and highly professional staff – all right in the centre of one of Britain's biggest cities. There were hundreds of bikes on display and courteous, switched on sales staff: in fact, state of the art for 2020.

What was more impressive was this took place at a time when most bike dealerships were still stuck in an era where

the owner wore oily overalls, dangled a cigarette from his mouth, and the bikes were piled up in a corner, inaccessible to customers.

Steve was not anti-Japanese. Rather, he was just pro something else – preferring to go his own way. Following the demise of the British bike industry, he turned to the Italians to provide sales. And he really did shift some bikes! The British Ducati importers had brought 120 examples of the first 750 Ducati twin into the country – and Sports Motorcycles sold 60 of them.

Steve was heavily involved in racing, and in 1977, with his rider Roger Nicholls, had come within seconds of winning the first Formula One TT when the race was stopped on the third lap because of appalling weather.

Steve said: "The weather had improved since the start of the race but Honda feared their bike would not last the race and so they lobbied the ACU (who were the governing body for the race) that it was too dangerous to continue.

"In my opinion, stopping the race was not legitimate, but only Honda knew what was happening. So, while our team took a careful, thorough pit stop, based on three more laps of racing, Honda rushed out Phil Read knowing the race would be over at the end of the next lap."

Steve was not happy at the way the race had been stopped, with only Honda aware of the organiser's decision, and felt he had been robbed of a rightful win – even if the letter of the regulations had been followed.

At the British GP, held in August of that year at Silverstone, he was introduced to Mike Hailwood who, completely out of character, was extremely unhappy. Mike had approached

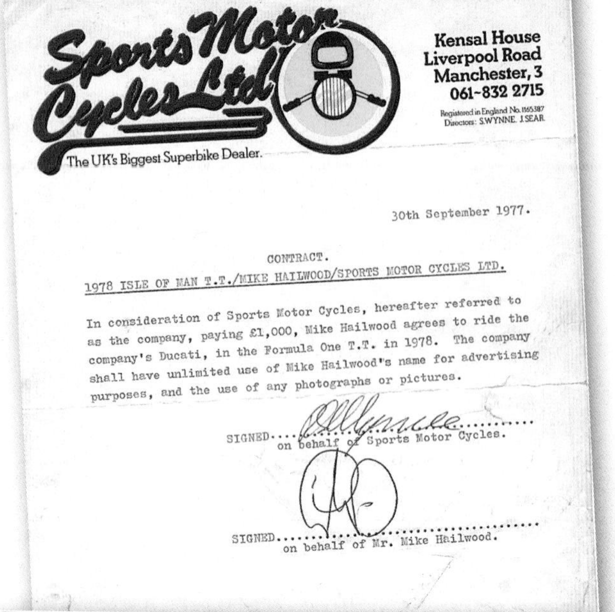

Sports Motor Cycles Ltd

The UK's Biggest Superbike Dealer.

Kensal House
Liverpool Road
Manchester, 3
061-832 2715

Registered in England No. 1165387
Directors: S.WYNNE. J.SEAR.

30th September 1977.

CONTRACT.

1978 ISLE OF MAN T.T./MIKE HAILWOOD/SPORTS MOTOR CYCLES LTD.

In consideration of Sports Motor Cycles, hereafter referred to as the company, paying £1,000, Mike Hailwood agrees to ride the company's Ducati, in the Formula One T.T. in 1978. The company shall have unlimited use of Mike Hailwood's name for advertising purposes, and the use of any photographs or pictures.

SIGNED............................
on behalf of Sports Motor Cycles.

SIGNED............................
on behalf of Mr. Mike Hailwood.

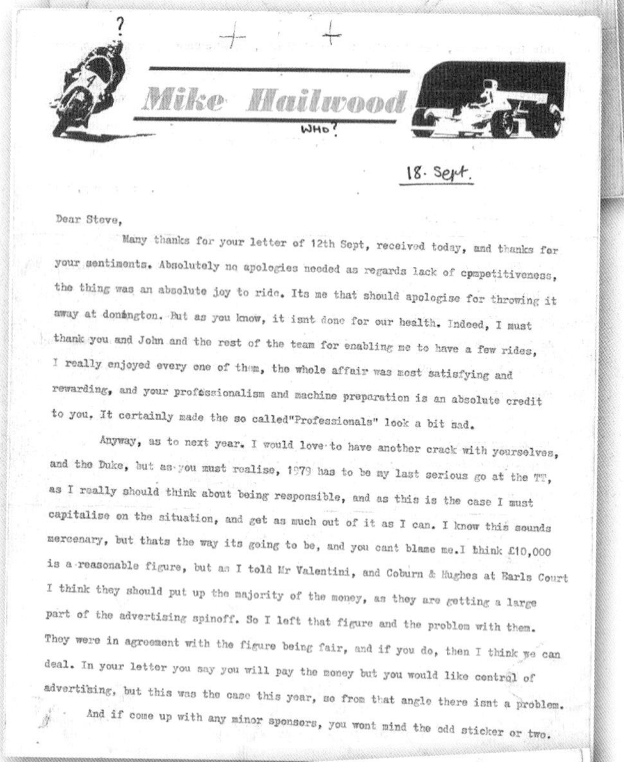

?

Mike Hailwood

WHO?

18. Sept.

Dear Steve,

Many thanks for your letter of 12th Sept, received today, and thanks for your sentiments. Absolutely no apologies needed as regards lack of cpmpetitiveness, the thing was an absolute joy to ride. Its me that should apologise for throwing it away at donington. But as you know, it isnt done for our health. Indeed, I must thank you and John and the rest of the team for enabling me to have a few rides, I really enjoyed every one of them, the whole affair was most satisfying and rewarding, and your professionalism and machine preparation is an absolute credit to you. It certainly made the so called"Professionals" look a bit sad.

Anyway, as to next year. I would love to have another crack with yourselves, and the Duke, but as you must realise, 1979 has to be my last serious go at the TT, as I really should think about being responsible, and as this is the case I must capitalise on the situation, and get as much out of it as I can. I know this sounds mercenary, but thats the way its going to be, and you cant blame me.I think £10,000 is a reasonable figure, but as I told Mr Valentini, and Coburn & Hughes at Earls Court I think they should put up the majority of the money, as they are getting a large part of the advertising spinoff. So I left that figure and the problem with them. They were in agreement with the figure being fair, and if you do, then I think we can deal. In your letter you say you will pay the money but you would like control of advertising, but this was the case this year, so from that angle there isnt a problem.

And if come up with any minor sponsors, you wont mind the odd sticker or two.

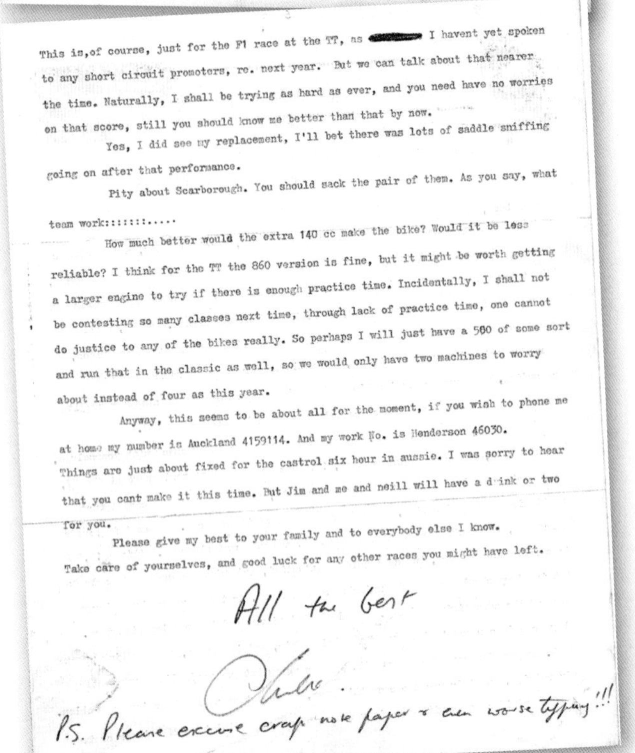

This is,of course, just for the F1 race at the TT, as [redacted] I havent yet spoken to any short circuit promoters, re. next year. But we can talk about that nearer the time. Naturally, I shall be trying as hard as ever, and you need have no worries on that score, still you should know me better than that by now.

Yes, I did see my replacement, I'll bet there was lots of saddle sniffing going on after that performance.

Pity about Scarborough. You should sack the pair of them. As you say, what team work::::::::.....

How much better would the extra 140 cc make the bike? Would it be less reliable? I think for the TT the 860 version is fine, but it might be worth getting a larger engine to try if there is enough practice time. Incidentally, I shall not be contesting so many classes next time, through lack of practice time, one cannot do justice to any of the bikes really. So perhaps I will just have a 500 of some sort and run that in the classic as well, so we would only have two machines to worry about instead of four as this year.

Anyway, this seems to be about all for the moment, if you wish to phone me at home my number is Auckland 4159114. And my work No. is Henderson 46030. Things are just about fixed for the castrol six hour in aussie. I was sorry to hear that you cant make it this time. But Jim and me and neill will have a drink or two for you.

Please give my best to your family and to everybody else I know.

Take care of yourselves, and good luck for any other races you might have left.

All the best

Mike.

P.S. Please excuse crap note paper & even worse typing!!!

Honda for a ride for the 1978 season and was told he was too old and past competing at top level.

Steve explains: "It was a meeting of two upset parties: us because we felt we had been cheated–and Mike because he felt slighted."

Mike agreed to ride for Sports Motorcycles for the whole season for £1,000 – and that's not a misprint!

Even this was a pay rise because, originally, Hailwood had offered to ride for free and enter anonymously under the nom de guerre of Edgar Jessop, asking only for a bike.

It was only later, when Hailwood's friend and manager Ted McCauley talked him into making the comeback public, that it was felt necessary to formalise the contract between Mike and Sports Motorcycles.

Steve said: "I wrote the contract, not a lawyer, on a single sheet of paper and the sum was very nominal for a rider of his immense status.

To emphasise this point, the following year Honda offered to buy out Mike's contract from me, for a package deal amounting to around £100,000."

Steve ordered three Formula One bikes from Ducati. One was to be for Mike; the second one for Roger Nicholls; and the third was paid for by Mike's friend Jim Scaysbrook, from Australia.

NCR were, de facto, the official Ducati race machine supplier – although an independent company, based virtually next to Ducati in Bologna.

The bikes arrived, absolutely on time, in October 1977 – and this in itself was a shock to Steve, who was well used to relaxed Italian delivery schedules.

Steve takes up the story: "The bikes were absolutely beautiful – milled levers, drilled sprockets, the full works, but unfortunately, most of it was polish and show.

"I said to them: 'Look, you know that if you shot-peened parts they would be ten times stronger than polishing'.

"And they said to me: 'Steve you don't understand the customers' minds. They want to show all their friends what they have paid for – and polishing shows, but shot peening doesn't look nearly so good'!

"But the bikes were basically right and, better still, I knew how to get them absolutely right."

He continued: "Cook Neilson sent me some really trick pistons from America, but I wasn't 100% happy with them so I got Fred Hadley at Omega Pistons, in Halesowen, to make me some.

"The gearbox on all the Ducati race bikes was notoriously fragile so I got a set of unhardened and unmachined pinions from Ducati – and Mike Hewland, who owned Hewland Gearboxes, machined and hardened them to my specification.

"This was where the Hailwood connection was useful. Mike Hewland made all the F1 car gearboxes and he was a mate of Mike's from when Hailwood had raced cars.

"Things were going well but I had to take the bikes out of Sports Motorcycles' workshop and to my garage at home because they were distracting my mechanics from their normal jobs – and they needed to work on customers' bikes to pay the wages. I built the Hailwood bike on my own – and outside works time, too.

"I had a huge amount of help from my sales director John Sears, who took a lot of the strain in dealing with the press and public interest. This freed me to get on with the bikes. John also had valuable experience of the Isle of Man as a Manx GP rider himself so he really understood the needs of the media."

The first shakedown test at the Oulton Park circuit, which was quite near to the Sports Motorcycles shop in Manchester, went very well. Hailwood was happy enough with the bike, but it was the performance of the Dunlop tyres that really had Mike ecstatic. In the 11 years he had been away from bike racing, tyre technology had undergone exponential progress and this really fired Hailwood up.

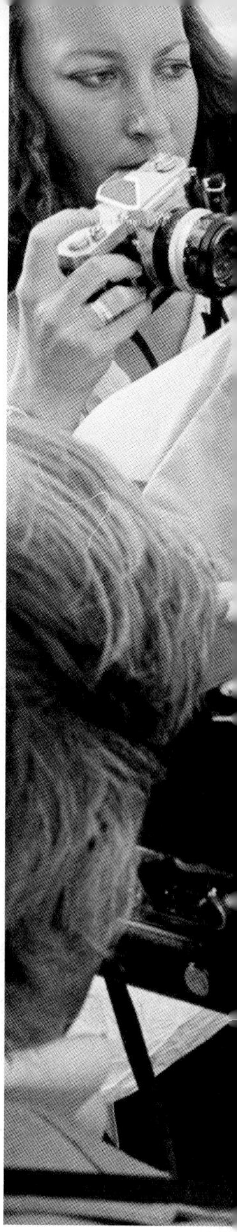

At this point, it is important to realise just how delightfully amateurish the Sports Motorcycles' effort was in some ways. Steve set off for the TT as chief mechanic, team manager and pick-up driver. Three race bikes went on the trailer – and another three in the pick-up, along with all the tools and spares.

Steve takes up the story again: "To be honest, it was just another TT. You were always late for the TT, and you always wanted another week to prepare, but there was no sense of history being made because Mike was the most laid back, relaxed person in the world.

"His attitude spread to the whole team and we were able to smile at his terrible development skills – and they were shocking.

"The truth is that Mike was so incredibly good he could just ride round problems as if they didn't exist. He could ride anything very fast. It didn't matter if the bike was good, bad or indifferent, he could just get on it and be faster than anyone else.

"What he didn't have were the skills to help to suggest what improvements could be made to a bike – and he didn't have the interest either.

"As an example, he never knew how many gears the Ducati had until the Post-TT meeting at Mallory Park. For the whole of the TT he thought the bike had a four speed 'box, instead of the five it really had, because he could never be bothered to remember what gear he was in.

"He really was incredibly laid back and easy to please. In practice for the TT he commented that the suspension was too hard until we realised that, in fact, it was too soft and Mike was bottoming the Girling units out everywhere.

"To be honest it was just another TT. You were always late for the TT, and you always wanted another week to prepare, but there was no sense of history being made because Mike was the most laid back, relaxed person in the world."

"But he was a complete and utter genius on the bike and understood racing perfectly. In practice he said: 'Steve, this is really easy. I am only cruising and I know I can beat Phil (Read) on the Honda (which was a full factory entry)'."

He continued: "There was a huge amount of attention on Mike but as far as we were concerned everything was just so relaxed and happy. He was the easiest rider in the world to work with.

"Everything was going really well but I was receiving a lot of hostile comments from Hailwood fans for providing a bike on which he was risking his reputation and his life.

"I received mail and 'phone calls from people who thought I shouldn't be giving a bike to Hailwood so he could kill himself. This was a problem in having a rider who was literally loved by his fans.

"I was really confident – but I did sometimes think about what could go wrong. And at the TT there are plenty of opportunities for a real disaster.

"I'm also useless at providing what sponsors want. If a sponsor gave me £100 then I wanted to spend £99 on the bike and £1 on the corporate hospitality, rather than the other way round, which sponsors rightly expect.

"I thought sponsorship was to enable us to do a better job racing instead of spending most of the money on cham-▸

pagne and all the other peripheral bits and pieces which sponsors want.

"So, I just got on with the bike and let Mike do the talking on the circuit.

"We did have factory personnel from Ducati with us, but they never touched the bike. I paid for their hotel because I thought I would get some first-class technical help from Ducati the following year – I never did – and later in the week, they nearly brought the whole show down.

"I also had some help from Pat Slyn of Coburn and Hughes, the British Ducati importer, and this was useful for doing the little jobs that take so much time at a race meeting.

"But mainly it was me and Mike: club racing really."

Steve added: "Our main opposition was from Read and Honda. Whenever Mike came out, everyone would cheer and when Phil appeared they would boo.

"Phil didn't help matters by facing the crowd down and giving them the 'V' whenever he could – but we were having a great time.

"In fact, I admire Phil as a real motorcycle racer. He isn't everyone's cup of tea, but he never did me any harm, and I wore a Phil Read t-shirt during the Formula One race.

"We only had one problem during practice, with an ignition box which failed, but otherwise everything was great and I didn't feel under any pressure – until the night before the race.

"There were all the factory blokes, and Coburn and Hughes' staff, and the Ducati people were getting really worried that the engine in the bike had done too many miles. They had been breaking engines in endurance racing and with Mike going so well they were nervous wrecks over the motor I had built.

"In the end, I cracked and gave in and I put a spare motor in the bike that they had shipped in at the last minute from Italy. It was nearly the worst thing I ever did."

Steve continued: "The race went perfectly with Mike leading from the start and chasing Phil down on the roads, until the Honda engine gave up.

"It was only afterwards that I realised what had been achieved and that is why I had so little in the way of memorabilia. We'd just gone to the TT to win a race with a good rider, done the job – and that was as far as it went."

"Mike crossed the line and then parked the bike up at the end of the pit lane. Everyone was going mad and I went to get the bike.

"The chief scrutineer came to me and said: 'The bike won't start will it'? I told him of course it would and he looked me in the eyes and said: 'Look I'm certain it won't start, got it'?

"We had been having trouble with getting the bike under 115dba all week, and the scrutineer knew if he noise-tested the bike, as he was supposed to do, it would be around 120dba and he would have been the man who had to exclude Hailwood. There was no way that he was going to do this – no way!

"But the big shock came when we got the bike back to Manchester. As Mike crossed the line, the bevel gear broke, which was quite common on the 860 race engines. You have to remember this was a 226-mile race, and had it given up 100 yards earlier, this would have been one of the great failures in motorcycling history – and 100 yards is not much in such a long race.

"It was only afterwards that I realised what had been achieved and that is why I had so little in the way of memorabilia. We'd just gone to the TT to win a race with a good rider – and that was as far as it went."

Steve concluded: "At the end of the season, I sold the bike to a Japanese collector for £5,000, which I thought was a good price because we'd used the bike all season, and I'd got my money back. It was great.

"In 1998, I was the under bidder when the bike came up for sale in Los Angeles. I gave up at $150,000, so maybe £5,000 wasn't such a good price after all.

"Now the bike is owned by Lawrence Auriana, an Italian car and bike collector, but I still look after it, and whenever the bike is run, part of the contract for it appearing is I have to be with the bike – and I can't ask for more than that." ◆

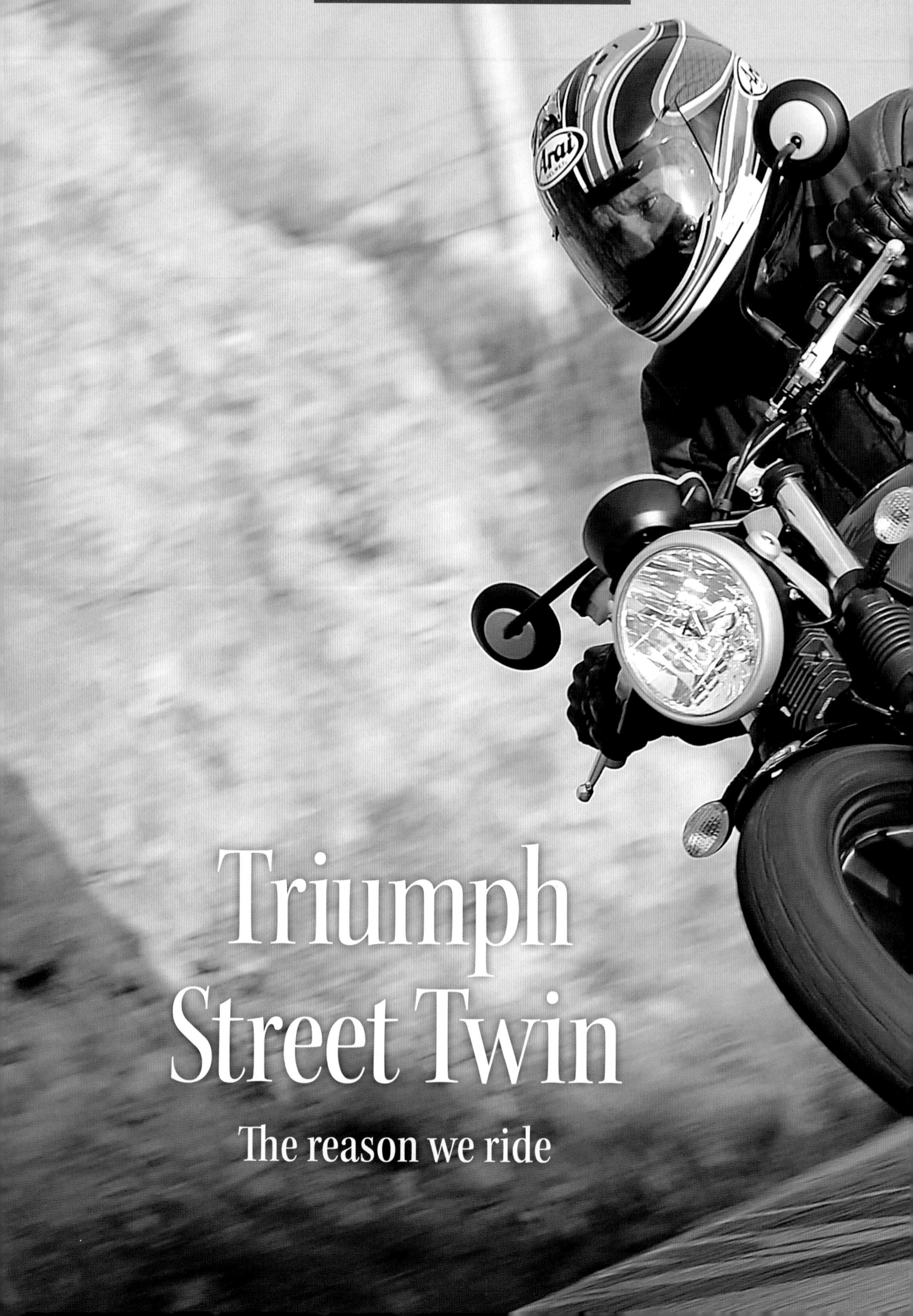

# Triumph Street Twin

## The reason we ride

**Miles Perkins (left) and Stuart Wood (right).**

"We didn't want riders who were very skilled getting off the Street Twin, yawning, looking at their watch and wondering if there was anything good on the telly."

**Left:**
**The Street Twin really is a handsome motorcycle and a true grandchild of the original Meriden Twins.**

**Above**
**Sohc 900cc engine really hits the sweet spot. Clearly, it could only be a twin.**

AT FIRST glance you might wonder why Triumph's smallest capacity and the factory's most affordable retro bike – I'll avoid the word 'cheap' for fear of a team of big blokes from Hinckley visiting me one night for a quiet chat in the back of their van – should appear in a book about classic superbikes.

The Street Twin's big brother, the Thruxton R, would be an obvious choice for this book because it has every toy in the retro box, but – if you didn't know better – you might think that the Street Twin is a bit ordinary. This would be an unfortunate mistake to make because the bike is one of the cleverest pieces of engineering to leave Triumph.

It's not only me who thinks this. The Street Twin is Triumph's best-selling retro bike, and the demand is really impressive. At the time of writing this chapter, 22,475 Street Twins have left Triumph dealers' showrooms and that, in the current highly competitive retro market, is a seriously large number.

Further, if you expect a discount on the Street Twin you'll be disappointed because these bikes sell at full MRRP all the time, and that's a rarity today.

Better still from Triumph's point of view is 90% of Street Twins are individualised by their buyers, with the addition of some of the 450 manufacturer approved accessories. It's a particularly clever pitch because a lot of the options are fitted by the dealers as part of the overall package and so don't affect the bike's warranty. What a smart, safe way to customise your bike.

The Bonneville family, of which the Street Twin is the opening act, consumed a colossal amount of engineering time, effort and money – all of which was very demanding for a company of Triumph's size. The product line was four years in gestation and took the full-time efforts of 50 engineers in the design team alone.

Add to this the production engineers and the staff designing the 450 accessories that go with the bike and it becomes readily apparent this was a range Triumph had to get right: being merely very good wasn't going to be an option.

So what makes the Street Twin so clever? The man who really knows is Stuart Wood, Triumph's chief engineer in the advanced engineering division and a complete and utter motorcycling addict. This is the story from the inside.

"We didn't just decide one day that we needed a replacement for the original Bonneville, but it was starting to come up more and more in conversations. We could have got the Bonneville through the increasingly tighter Euro 4 emission regulations, but it was getting harder to do this with an air-cooled engine.

"We started to think about an air-/water-cooled engine for the new bikes but the design brief was really demanding. It wasn't just the engine either. We wanted to improve the whole bike whilst retaining the characteristics of the existing machine, which everyone loved.

"It was a very complicated design challenge and this is what made it particularly interesting.

"The first problem was that the old Bonneville was loved by its owners and so we couldn't upset the existing customer base.

"We also wanted a machine which would appeal to riders who had just got their full motorcycle licence and didn't want an evil monster which was going to be too much for their first big bike."

He continues: "Then we were determined to have a bike which was fun for an expert, too. We didn't want riders who were very skilled getting off the Street Twin, yawning, looking at their watch and wondering if there was anything good on the telly.

"No – we were set on having a bike that, when you got off it, it was a disappointment that you had to stop riding – a bike where you thought, sod it, I'll just have another hour. ▸

"The package is light and manageable by a whole range of riders"

"Of course, this was a big wish list and there was another problem. It was no good having lots of very expensive fixes to achieve all these aims because the bike had to have a really attractive selling price that was highly affordable to a lot of customers.

"Instead of technical bling, we came up with some clever engineering fixes based on real world riding – and, more than anything else, the Street Twin is a real world bike.

"For example, we made the engine produce peak torque just in the rev range where most of us ride most of the time.

"On the launch, the results were fascinating. We had all these hard core journalists riding the bikes and the vast majority over-estimated the 55hp the engine produced because it felt it had much more power.

"Now, we've got even more power and torque and the engine is even nicer."

Stuart adds: "We also understood our customers on a very intimate level. No-one wants to drone down the motorway at 75mph with the fillings coming out of your teeth because the engine is vibrating. That's not involving; it's just a bad experience.

"But you do want to feel the engine when you accelerate away down a long, sweeping country lane. You want to know that you've got a big twin between your legs and not an electric scooter.

**1**
**Retro clock is effective and aesthetically pleasing. There's also a simple computer in there too.**

**2**
**Detail is lovely like these elegant headlamp brackets.**

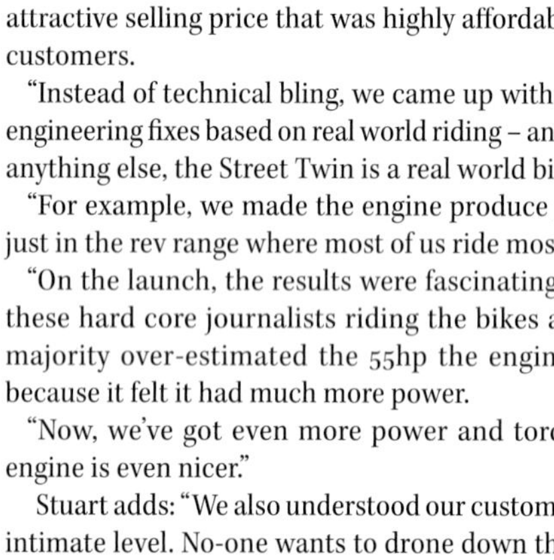

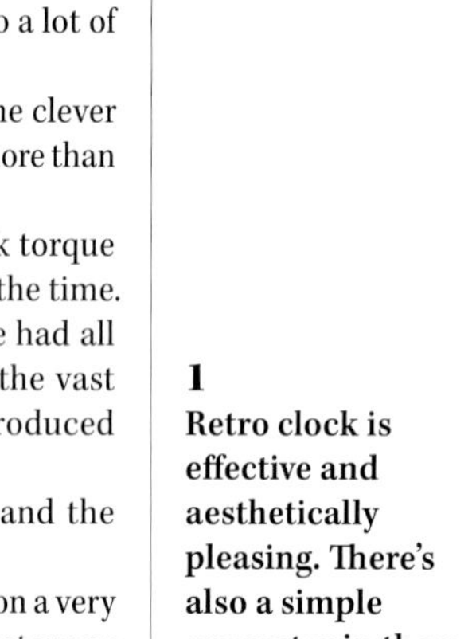

"So, we put a 270 degree crank in the engine which allows the rider to feel the firing pulses and also hear the induction roar – but only under hard acceleration.

"In terms of the steering geometry, we wanted the bike to have a neutral feel. For the less experienced, the Street Twin will never bite the rider, but you can also ride the wheels off it in complete safety.

"The final bit of the equation was to ensure that the ergonomics were right. The bike isn't intimidatingly high for shorter riders, and yet there is plenty of room, too.

"Before the launch, we were confident that we had got something special on our hands with the Street Twin, but by lunch-time we were certain. Bike journalists are not easy to impress and everyone was sitting down with a big smile.

"That made us very happy and very proud."

I was one of those happy journos, and Triumph had a particularly hard sell in my case. I'll be honest – I wasn't a fan of the original Hinckley Bonneville. I thought it was a dull lump, and I wouldn't give one the time of the day. For me, the Hinckley Bonneville also lacked integrity and I value honesty above all else in a motorcycle. Whether the bike is as amiable as a Labrador puppy or a psychopathic Rottweiler I am happy either way – providing it is what it is.

When the bike was launched, I was writing for an American website, and so I was sent out to ride the all new Street Twin, but I didn't lie awake at night dreaming about the assignment. Entry level bikes in a new model's range are rarely worth getting excited about.

The first thing that hit all the journos when we saw the bike on the evening before our test ride was, it was a lovely motorcycle. The Street Twin sat well in the sunshine and looked really, really nice. This is difficult to express in terms of steering head angles and wheelbases, but it just looked right – harmonious, purposeful and every inch an honest motorcycle.

The finish was spot on, too. If Triumph were chasing critical price points it didn't show in the fit and finish.

I was the fat, bald, old wrinkly in the press corps, and it was interesting to hear the younger journalists seeing those opportunities that slipped by me. There was an immediate response that the Street Twin was 'retro-chique' (I think that means when your waxed cotton jacket doesn't smell of sheep lanolin) and an immediate target for customising.

I liked the bike because it looked authentically classic – except there were no pools of oil under the test fleet and Triumph were quite confident all the bikes would start the following morning, without changing plugs or pushing.

Clearly, the bike had to be a parallel twin. You could hardly have a four-cylinder 'Bonnie', otherwise classic wrinklies like me would have marched over to Hinckley and burnt the factory down. Equally clearly, the engine needed to be compliant with all current and predicted emissions' regulations.

Triumph's solution to all these demands really is a lovely thing.

First, the new motor looks drop-dead gorgeous. It's not a 1958 Bonnie, but any proud grandparent would look at the widely splayed exhaust ports, with their finned clamps, and the motor's handsome angular lines and beam with pride. "Oh yes," they would coo, "that's my lovely little lad and doesn't he look just like his Grandad?" – which of course is completely and wholly true, because he does.

However, beneath the family good looks lies a very modern engine. The key thing is the new motor is partially water cooled. This is essential so the engine can be built to very tight tolerances to meet the regulators' demands. However, it is also genuinely air-cooled so the radiator is small and unobtrusive.

With 900cc in the toy box, there was no need to tune the engine to the ragged edge. Rather, Triumph could go for a single, over-head cam design, but with a unique form of eccentric cam to open the eight valves. The end result is only 55hp @ 5900rpm, but don't let this lead you astray. It's a very torquey motor making 59ft-lbs of torque at a mere 3230rpm so, in real life riding, there is plenty of practical, useable power. The current motors are even better with an extra 10hp, more torque and the ability to rev on another 500rpm.

Using a sohc design also makes the engine short – if you wanted to play fantasy engine building you could almost pretend it is a classic push-rod motor – and this allows the fuel tank to be low in the chassis, making the bike feel lighter than its already svelte 437lbs dry (198kg). Mass centralisation is just as important for a retro bike as it is for a MotoGP machine, and the bike really does feel very manageable.

What is clever is the bits you don't need to see are tucked away and out of sight. Take the dreaded catalyser as one example. Unless you are a journalist poking around on a launch you will never find the 'cat', it is hidden so well beneath the engine.

However, you will see the lovely, brushed stainless twin exhausts. They look and sound absolutely gorgeous, emitting a throaty rumble which would grace any 1960s sporting twin. Yet, the exhausts are completely legal because of the way exhaust noise levels are now measured, with the bike being tested under acceleration. Done this way, the torquey, low-revving Triumph can get away with making the sort of tenor music it should produce rather than being choked down to some sibilant rustling.

Because this is the happy-clappy, relaxed 21st century, the bike must have fuel injection and Triumph have absolutely nailed this with perfect fuelling from tickover all the way to when the rev limiter kicks in at 7,500rpm. ▸

**Below**
**Coming to a mountain road near you – for certain!**

The 84.6 x 80mm bore and stroke suits the engine perfectly. The cam profile, which Triumph spent an inordinate amount of time developing, is right on the money for its intended purpose.

The nasty, retina-loosening vibes of the good old days – and they really were bad – have been designed out by using a 270° firing configuration and twin counter balancers. This is conventional, modern engineering.

However, here's where the plot gets really interesting. Triumph has done much better than just ordinary, sound engineering. The motor does vibrate – but from the firing impulses. You can actually feel the bangs, albeit discreetly and in the background. They are a joy for anyone who really does believe in the two-wheeled horse and wants to feel its heart beating. I loved feeling the motor talking to me.

In real-life situations the power is ideal for its intended purpose, with plenty of urge right from the moment the throttle is opened. The clutch is sweet and light too with no grabbiness and the gearbox is positive, with five ideally spaced ratios. In fact, the whole package is so user friendly you could teach a new rider the first stages of the art of motorcycling.

Like the power plant, the chassis is much cleverer than it looks. It's a steel, twin- shock design, but with bracing tubes in front and behind the engine. This gives a taught, tight, modern feel which is very comfortable for another market sector Triumph are trying to attract – the super-sports rider, tired of battling with 175hp and the constant danger of having his licence removed for six months.

The front forks are excellent, but if I owned a Street Twin the first change I would make is to put some quality, after-market rear shocks on the bike because the standard Kayabas are only okay: nothing more. What's needed is a pair of Maxton gas shocks, which are the standard equipment for every serious classic racer in the world.

The front brake looks incredibly modest with a single, 310mm disc gripped by a Nissin 2-piston floating caliper, with ABS. Regardless of how it looks on paper, this is a seriously good anchor, and you will never need more power -- no matter if the Street Twin is fully loaded and carrying luggage. The rear brake sort of works, and is clearly there for legal reasons, but it isn't of much more than decorative value.

The ergonomics of the bike are excellent – absolutely first class. The seat height is low, and completely unintimidating, but the thin saddle is very comfortable – surprisingly so. On the launch, I rode with journalist Julia LaPalme and she was kind enough to give me some key female data – because this is another market sector Triumph is anxious to reach. Julia is 5ft 5in tall and has a 30in inside leg. She could place both feet on the ground without a problem.

**Inset**
**Julia LaPalme can reach the ground perfectly with a 30 inch inside leg**

**Above**
**One seriously handsome motorcycle.**

I am 6 inches taller and there was still plenty of room for me, plus spare room to stretch back. Anyone up to six feet and a bit will be fine. Overall, it is a seriously thoughtful piece of design and shows the care Triumph have taken over this project.

Within a few yards of setting off, you can't help but like the Street Twin. It's eager to please right from the off, and the bike is immediately involving. Other than lacking a tail to wag, it reminds me of my much lamented Collie bitch waiting by the back door when we were about to go for a walk.

There is a single, imitation analogue speedometer – it's really electronic – and discreetly hidden in there is information about average fuel consumption, current fuel consumption and miles to empty. However, this is not a bike to be ridden while playing about with electronic options. A Street Twin is more to be felt, rather than controlled with a Play Station console.

The reality is the bike must, absolutely must, be ridden in the lovely area between 3,000rpm and 6,000rpm. Below 2,500rpm the motor is asking for a few more revs to be comfortable and if it is buzzed hard it starts to get all grumbly and irritable. The Street Twin will manage nearly 50mph in first gear, so it is hardly an arthritic slug, but the motor doesn't like these revs.

At the other end of the scale, one of the Triumph test riders told me the Street Twin would run up to 110mph – but both he and the bike didn't like to be there.

We ambled along at 80mph on the Spanish motorways and the world was a wonderful place to be: effortless, involving and graceful.

The Street Twin is ludicrously light on fuel. Ridden very hard, as we did in the morning test session, the bike returned 55mpg. In the afternoon, riding the bike as it is intended to be used, 70mpg was showing on the computer all the time.

For some reason I don't fully understand, Triumph took us into the hills for some seriously spirited riding. I can report with complete honesty if you want to ride the Street Twin like Malcolm Uphill's 1969 Production TT-winning Bonneville then the bike is up to the job – as the wear on my toe sliders will verify.

I rode in second gear, using the engine as a rear wheel brake, and I had a great time. But here's the important thing: I had even more fun riding back to the hotel at a far gentler pace.

With the big twin burbling along at 3,500rpm (or so my bum-mounted rev counter reported back to me) in third and fourth gear, the Street Twin was a lovely place to be, and a wonderful reminder of why I am a motorcyclist and will be until my dying day. ◆

"The Street Twin was a lovely place to be and a wonderful reminder of why I am a motorcyclist - and will be until my dying day."

# Triton

Available in many flavours
from a shed near you

As the years go by, history is getting a little bit distorted – as it always has been. The end of the mighty BSA factory is always a hotly discussed affair among fans of classic bikes, but my memories of the event tend to be fairly accurate because at the moment the closure actually took place I was sat in my car in Golden Hillock Road, just outside the Small Heath factory, having barely made it out of the works when the chains went on the gates. If that isn't having first-hand knowledge, I'm not sure what is...

I'm also always slightly confused with the mods/rockers/café racer culture theme which is now so popular. To be clear, I have no problem with café racer bikes. In fact, one of my favourite motorcycles currently on sale is the Triumph Thruxton R – by far the best of all the 'retro caffs'.

I've also no issues with people dressing up and pretending to be something they're not. We spent two brilliant days at the Ribe Viking Village in Denmark this summer, where the re-enactors there take authenticity to a whole new level of realism: and I can say, with complete certainty, that Viking life was tough and unhygienic!

So, if anyone wants to dress up in a leather jacket and Brylcreem their hair, why not? It's when history is bent and squeezed to fit the myth that I become somewhat concerned.

Here are the facts. There were virtually no 'rockers' riding café racers in the 1960s – there really weren't. I would put money on there being fewer than 5,000 rockers in the whole of Britain. Of those who were part of this group, they were mainly centred on London. Hence, the seaside 'mods v rockers' riots of 1964 were clustered around the South Coast seaside towns.

At the time, I wasn't old enough to hold a licence, but I did hear gossip about a potential riot at Rhyl, on the North Wales coast, but there weren't enough mods or rockers for a decent battle so both sides had fish and chips together outside one of the arcades on the seafront!

The truth of the matter was there were more spectators at a big Oulton Park road race meeting, or an international motocross at Hatherton Hall or Hawkstone Park, than you would have got by press-ganging every rocker from Brighton to Blackpool into one location.

In my dreams, I didn't want to fight anyone – except, obviously, the Hun, with me flying a Spitfire – and especially not anyone who was riding anything with two wheels. My heroes were not some fag-smoking, leather jacket-wearing layabouts wearing silly caps with chains on – but Mike Hailwood, Jim Redman, Alan Shepherd and the other great road racers I idolised.

These were real people, and they rode real race bikes, on real tracks, and I ached to be one of them – not a fake wannabee.

The same applied to bikes. I did want a race bike on the road - but not a Triton or café racerised 350 Triumph. Most of all, I lusted after a Velocette Venom Clubman or, in a real extreme fantasy dream, a BSA Rocket Gold Star with a 190mm front brake and a few Eddie Dow bits.

As for Tritons, they were about, but weren't common. Further, Tritons tended to be built by people who could not afford a genuine bike so they were often strong contenders for Crufts rather than examples of impeccable engineering. This is not to say all Tritons were rough because there were some really nice machines put together, and I did like these. However, the central raison d'être of the bikes was they were cheap to make, using second-hand parts.

It's worth bearing mind how affordable bits were. A useable BSA or Triumph gearbox was anywhere between £5 and £10 and a pre-unit construction, fine-finned Triumph Tiger 100 engine perhaps twice that.

A complete Norton rolling chassis would have been £25. Even a Manx chassis, less the engine and gearbox, was only £150.

Because there was so much engineering still being done in Britain rear set footrests, brake pedals and all the other Triton bits and pieces invariably came as 'foreigners' – produced in works time with works material and paid for with a reciprocal favour or 'a drink'.

Again, for the sake of historical accuracy, there were commercially available parts from companies like Dresda Engineering and John Tickle, but these firms were supplying tiny quantities. The two big sellers I remember from later were Triton engine plates and swept back exhausts – both ▸

**1**
**Modern Tritons, like this superb French one, can be very chic retro.**

**2**
**A well built Triton is a handsome beast.**

**3**
**Instrumentation on a Triton should be minimalist. Clip on handlebars look cool but will kill you in terms of comfort.**

of these items being tricky to make at home or get done at work.

The best Tritons really were nice motorcycles, and I both admired and liked these – it was just that these high-class thoroughbreds were in the minority compared to the mass of mongrels that were knocked up in garden sheds.

Now things are very different. Firstly, Tritons have become main stream and seem to have found a niche in the custom market. This is why you now see so many Tritons in utterly pristine, almost unridden condition. Rock up at a show with a real Triton from 1965, complete with a misaligned front mudguard, dog-rough fibreglass fuel tank held on with elastics and an incontinent Triumph engine leaking oil all over the floor and you will probably be sent somewhere well out of sight – behind the toilets and next to the rubbish skips.

In stark contrast, 21st century Tritons are cool and, I have to say, there are some wonderful examples about which fill me with admiration.

In the best middle class manner, Tritons are now also very much like wine. Answer this one simple question.

Do you like wine?

Wine?

What wine? ▸

3

Norton

**Above**
**The Triton in our feature being ridden by owner Ean Lewin at a street race.**

**Left**
**A pre-unit construction 650 Triumph in a Featherbed frame - the definitive Triton.**

"Do you honestly and truthfully want to track parade, or even race, your Triton - or will the bike be a Sunday-only, day out machine?"

Do you prefer to get hammered on a Calais booze superstore 'Special', at £5 a gallon, or perhaps you prefer to sip a Saint-Émilion Premier Grand Cru from Jacques Thienpont – yours for a highly affordable £1200 a bottle – but the lingering tannins are worth every penny, so I am reliably informed.

So, at one end of the market there are Tritons built from a rolling chassis that began life housing Manx Norton engines, and which carry Manx brakes, forks and fuel tanks, and at the other end of the scale reside Tritons whose predecessors bore only the loosest genetic affiliation to Norton's GP heritage.

Let's start at the very beginning. The two McCandless brothers are toiling away in Belfast at the end of the Second World War. Both Rex and Cromie were excellent racers, with Cromie the more talented, but Rex a gifted, self-taught engineer.

Riding on the Ulster road circuits, Rex was unhappy with the handling of his 500 Triumph because he felt, correctly, that the frame flexed to a dangerous degree. Henceforth, frame flexing dominated McCandless' thinking in terms of frame design. He vastly improved the Triumph with a neat, perimeter-framed special named the 'Benial' (Gaelic for beast) which, remarkably for the time, had swinging arm suspension with rear dampers from a Citroen car.

While Rex was having great success with his Triumph special, Norton were facing problems, both with suspect handling of their 'Garden Gate' racers and, for added fun, the frames were breaking, too.

The solution was to pay McCandless £1 per hour – but with the savage caveat Norton actually had to accept the Ulsterman's ideas as being worth considering before he got a penny – to design and build what was to become the iconic 'Featherbed' frame.

The new frame was a full, duplex design for two reasons. Firstly, as I have noted, McCandless' thinking was dominated by the desire to avoid frame flex. He was, sensibly, obsessed with keeping the front and rear wheels in line. The second critical factor was the height of the Norton 30M Manx engine.

At the top of the motor is a high cam box and at the bottom a deeply finned sump. The 30M also has very wide fins on both the cylinder barrel and head, as befits a Grand Prix engine, which was expected to run flat out in the hottest conditions.

To get this tall, wide engine into his new frame, McCandless splayed both the top and bottom rails out into what looks not unlike a large, rectangular box. Now, the cam box could be squeezed in between the top rails and the sump dangled out through the bottom ones.

Of course, this large empty space has proved to be a sheer delight for specials' builders ever since and there is almost nothing which hasn't been squeezed into the vast, and easily accessible, areas inside a Featherbed.

For Triton constructors, the Featherbed is a dream – lots of room and, potentially at least, jolly good handling.

The problem is Featherbed frames come in a huge range of flavours from the lightweight, Reynolds 531 Manx frame, complete with an oval swinging arm, to some real doggy examples rescued from a derelict Norton ES2, found decaying in a shed. ▸

Move over Mike Hailwood...

"Perhaps you prefer to sip a Saint-Emilion Premier Grand Cru from Jacques Thienpont. Yours for a highly affordable £1200 a bottle - and the lingering tannins are worth every penny, so I am reliably informed."

The same applies to the forks, tanks and hubs. At the most desirable end it really was possible to buy a Manx rolling chassis for almost nothing in the early-1970s and this then formed the ultimate basis for a Triton. A Manx chassis will have, ideally at least, a double-sided 7in front brake and the iconic Manx conical rear hub. The front forks will be 'Short' Norton Roadholders, and the alloy fuel and oil tanks will be lifted directly from a Manx. These were the Tritons I got caned for drawing in my jotter – and quite right, too – and which I liked so much as a baby journalist.

The problem is if thoroughbred Manx Tritons are not exactly unicorns, or dentally superior chickens, then they are near relatives. For example, an original, uncracked Manx rear hub is now worth £1500, so they tend not to be found on specials. Expect to pay a solid £10,000 for an unbent Manx rolling chassis in useable condition. Also, bear in mind the recommended working life for a Reynolds tube Featherbed was three years – and the last original Norton-made frame left the factory in 1963!

Go down a notch and it is possible to construct a really nice imitation Manx for a lot less money. All the Featherbed chassis have the same geometry so they all steer and handle just as well, and it is possible to do a lot of 'tribute' engineering on a budget.

For example, a Manx conical hub can be replicated with a BSA Group item from the last few years of production. Fibreglass tanks or, better still, replica Manx alloy tanks can be sourced and will be fresh, new and safe.

While not exactly brilliant, a BSA Group conical front hub can be made to work and there are zillions around at autojumbles for not much money. If you want to believe a BSA Group conical hub is a Manx or Oldani race item then you can. After all, fantasies never hurt anyone much – unless they involved whistling the Horst Wessel Song and flicking through maps of Poland.

Clearly, a Triumph engine is the power plant of choice, but the variation in this respect is just as wide as it is with chassis. The supreme Triton motor is a pre-unit Bonneville engine with a Norton gearbox, belt drive and NEB dry clutch behind it. The late Norton 'box is the best from this era and the clutch is excellent, too. However, the Triumph gearbox is perfectly okay.

What you put into the engine is a matter of choice – and common sense. You have to ask yourself the key question – and answer it honestly. It's this. Do I honestly and truthfully want to track parade, or even race, my Triton, or will the bike be a Sunday-only, day out machine whose highlight of the year would be the Classic Bike Show at Stafford?

If you want to take the bike out on the track, you will need a nine-stud cylinder head, dynamically balanced crank, decent cams, Wiseco high compression pistons, a pair of carbs and properly swept back pipes. Electronic ignition, ideally hiding

inside a reproduction Lucas K2FR magneto body, is highly desirable. In reality, a Triton in this specification will be a road-registered race bike.

Built like this, the best Tritons are spectacular race bikes, and in fact Dave Degens, the world's best Triton builder, won the Barcelona 24-hour race in 1965 riding one of his own bikes.

Alternatively a late, alloy head, pre-unit Thunderbird spec engine will provide all the power you could possibly want and/or need and will be infinitely nicer to ride on the road.

As for the rest of a Triton, there is a quasi-religious check list of things you must have because all Tritons aspire to be road racing machines. So clip-on handlebars, a chromed headlamp and rear-set footrests are essential formal dress for any self-respecting café racer. Swept back exhaust pipes terminating in absorption silencers which look gorgeous – but which only make a nod towards noise reduction – are also essential.

It's almost impossible to answer the question: "What's it like to ride a Triton?" for all the reasons discussed so far. A good, 650 Triton with a well-sorted Bonneville production racing engine and decent brakes is all you would ever need for fast parades. Featherbed frames are always stiff and precise and now, with modern race tyres, they are also more forgiving than previously.

So, with a £12,000 budget, you could build a really nice track/parade/show/occasional Sunday morning run bike.

**1**
**Brian Sadler on his Dresda Triton battles with Tom Holubowicz and his 350 Honda.**

**2**
**Michael Avery 1957 650 Triton. Good Tritons are seen on the track.**

**3**
**Mick Collins 750 Triton uses a unit engine and a Grimeca front brake - often favoured by Triton builders.**

The downside, and it really is a problem because most Triton fans are no longer in their late-teens and early-20s, is that the clip-on handlebars and rear set footrests will cripple you – they really, truly will.

I have spent a life-time riding race bikes and so I can manage being draped across the tank in a pose which, on the road, would look silly to the point of having a call from your local psychiatric clinic offering you an immediate appointment. Even on a race track, I can barely get off our Seeley Suzuki at the end of a 20-minute race.

The mere thought of riding a road bike with the weight resting entirely on my multiple broken wrists, and with my knackered knees bent double, is horrendous.

A better set up is to have some neat, short 'bars which are higher than the fork yokes and footrests, and in the normal Norton position for their road bikes. A Triton done like this is not nearly as sexy looking as a race replica, but it is vastly more useable.

You can have an awful lot of fun building a really eye-catching Triton, which will also work in the real world – whether that world is the track or the road – but, more than anything else, you will need a serious reality check before either beginning work on the project or building a completed bike.

For information contact the genius of Triton building which is: Dave Degens Dresda Autos: www.dresda.co.uk

Telephone: 01293 871887 ◆

# The Last Works BSA

## A fairy tale for grown-ups

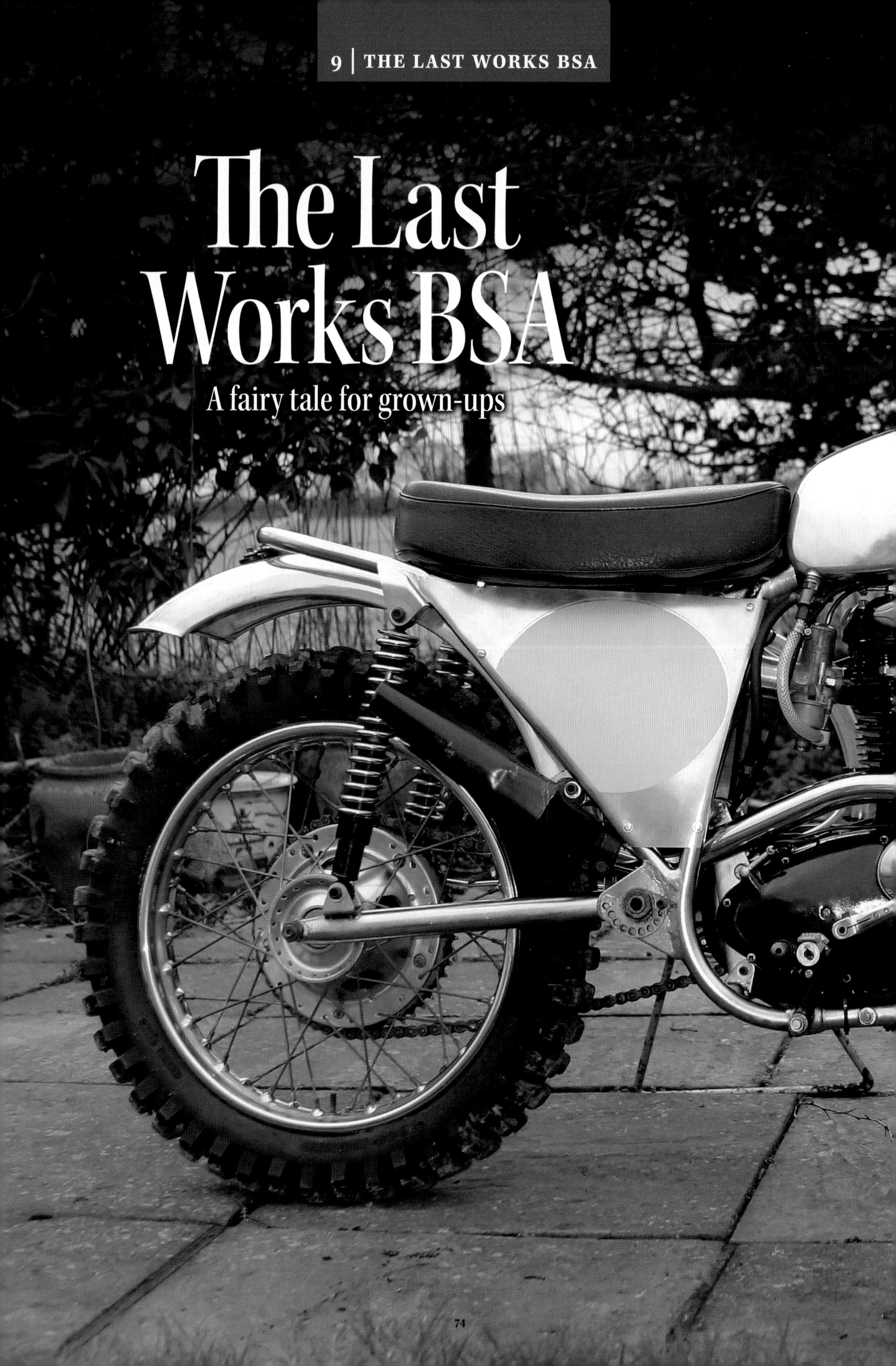

EVERYONE in the classic scene knows at least one good tale about some lad who found a Manx Norton in a shed and bought it for scrap value because the owner needed the room to breed budgies. They are good stories but, invariably, it is always a friend of a friend of someone's cousin. This story is almost identical except that in this case, it is perfectly true. I know because I was, almost to my embarrassment, BSA's last works rider.

For a factory of BSA's status, which had some of the world's greatest riders under its banner, having a clubman racer of no great merit compete with a fully supported works machine might seem inconceivable, but it really did happen.

Like all good fairy tales, some parts of the story have become shrouded in the mists of time but on this occasion, the fog comes from an unusual source. If you read any of the marque histories they will relate the end of the BSA competition history something like this.

In July 1971, the factory was under tremendous pressure to save money and the competition shop was an easy and obvious target. It was helped on its way to the guillotine by the fact that racing manager Brian Martin was not a particularly political animal and had not overtly courted friends in the BSA hierarchy. Thus, when senior management described the 'comp shop' fitters as "professional thieves" – a comment based on their willingness to liberate parts needed for racing from the production line – it becomes clear there were those who were more than glad to see the back of racing activities at Small Heath.

The better books will go on to say that a few staff were kept on until November to clear up and then the contents of the race shop were sold to Vale-Onslow in Birmingham while Alan Clews bought much of the B.50 motocross racing stock and, later, many of the jigs and tools. Thus BSA motocross history was neatly ended.

Unfortunately for historians, events are never really neat and tidy and have a habit of doing the most inconsistent things. Enter then Frank Melling: young and inexperienced as a journalist, but in the powerful position of writing two columns for influential American magazines–and, most crucially of all, a fanatically keen motocross rider.

In those days, it was very unusual for a journalist to race as well as write, and other than an occasional article by Peter Fraser, who was a trials rider, and sometime scrambler Gavin Trippe, motocross track tests were rare. By contrast, I was competing at least once a week, and although only a competent centre runner, I was deeply involved in the sport.

Given this background, I was desperately keen to get my hands on a B.50 MX to test, since this bike, in the hands of the BSA factory team, had been a formidable tool.

The B.50 was the last of the line of famous unit construction engines that dominated British motocross to an extent that is hard to comprehend now. With a blood line that is arguably traceable all the way back to the BSA. C15 – but certainly a direct descendant of the C15's bigger brother, the 350cc B40 – the B.50 was an engine that had evolved, rather than being the product of a designer's drawing board. This one fact was to be the source of the B.50's strengths–and its weaknesses.

Brian Martin began developing this engine for motocross in 1961, and by the following year it had grown into the 421cc motor that took Jeff Smith to the 1964 world championship. Although around 10 bhp down on the old DBD 34 Gold Star, and just as much on the Lito and Matchless opposition, the 421cc BSA was, at 228 lbs (103kgs), breathtakingly light. It was designed to last for just 90 minutes – two 45-minute Grand Prix races–and nothing more. At the end of this period, the engine was often near death. BSA works mechanic, Fred Barlow, remembers stripping engines where the main bearings could be pushed out of the crankcases with thumb pressure alone.

This was to be the hallmark of the whole unit construction racing engine programme. Weight pared down to the limit; instant, vicious power right from the moment the engine fired – and just enough reliability to win a Grand Prix.

The 421 grew into a 441cc engine for the following year, and again Smith took the world championship – on this occasion after an epic battle with Rolf Tibblin. Celebrating this famous victory, the factory launched the B44GP Victor in November 1964 – a true replica of Smithy's GP bike complete with a Reynolds 531 frame, but using an alloy, instead of magnesium, engine. The Victor was an instant, and sustained, sales success, but its progeny, in the form of the B.44 road and trail bikes, were less so. First last and middle, the B44 was a racing engine and its qualities could not be easily transferred to road motors.

Then came the great titanium disaster. In an effort to take the triple-crown, the BSA management launched into a no-holds barred total warfare campaign, the like of which no British factory had ever attempted. Titanium frames were commissioned from the Speedwell Gear Company – one of the few firms in the world who could work the material effectively – and new 490cc engines were employed. These had magnesium crankcases, rocker boxes and side-cases.

The cylinder barrels were light alloy with chrome bores. Titanium (Ti) rockers and connecting rods were used, along with a dural clutch. The timing gears and engine sprockets were fabricated from Ti, too. However, these attempts at the ultimate in lightness were only the beginning. Dunlop even rolled special Ti wheel rims and, initially, the fork legs and fork crowns were fabricated from Ti and a rear disc brake was employed – decades before the Japanese 're-invented' the idea. ▸

**Left**
**B50 MX engine in all its glory.**

**Above**
**Frank Melling - 500 Works BSA.**

"The B50 was the last of the line of famous, unit construction engines that dominated British motocross to an extent that is hard to comprehend now."

With so many brand-new concepts, there just had to be problems–and there were: and by the van-load, too. The frames flexed excessively and then cracked just behind the left-hand side footrest mounting and the main bearings turned in the crankcases while the fully floating rear disc brake sheared its mounting bolts. And that was just a start.

Within a few months, the project had been abandoned but it was not, contrary to current popular myth, a total loss. For a start, it was found that the bike could be made virtually as light – and much more reliable, with better handling, by using a Reynolds 531 frame. Thus, the following year, John Banks' GP bike weighed in at 223 lbs (101kgs) with a steel frame and a, by now, fully sorted magnesium engine. And if 223lbs (101kgs) doesn't sound light, it is literally only a few pounds heavier than a 175cc BSA Bantam, but with the power of a good DBD 34 Gold Star engine.

The Ti-framed bike did eventually prove to be a winner in the hands of Jeff Smith when he defeated the toughest of opposition to take the 250cc BBC Grandstand Trophy in 1967. In this guise, the Ti frame carried a beautiful little centre-plug head, Barracuda engine, giving just under 24bhp at 7,000rpm, breathing through a 1¼in Amal GP carburettor. This might not sound like a lot of power when compared to modern two-stroke engines but was well competitive with the Greeves, Dots and more importantly, the twin-port CZ's of the day.

Not only did the baby BSA knock out the power but it was actually lighter than the two-strokes, weighing in at an astounding 194lbs (88kgs).

If the Barracuda had a fault it was the lack of bottom-end power. Smithy was quoted in the press as saying: "The throttle stays wide open. I change speed by going up or down the 'box."

The same could not be said for the B.50 engines. They all made brutal power right off the throttle stop and there was a constant search for even more torque. The overwhelming reason for this was drive – or rather the lack of it. It has to be remembered that in 1969, rear suspension was still virtually non-existent. A good motocross machine had four

**1**
**The little bay inside Cyril Halliburn's Quality Control department was where BSA's 'grey' racing projects took place in the factory's dying days.**

**2**
**Cyril Halliburn with the ill-fated BSA Speedway bike. Cyril doted on the young Frank Melling.**

**3**
**Melling's works BSA after the first test session. It was a full-on, hand- built factory special and Frank loved it.**

inches of travel controlled by poorly damped Girling oil dampers. A dreadful, uncompetitive bike had four inches of travel controlled by the same Girlings – there just wasn't an alternative.

The tyres were equally bad. There was slightly more choice in that one could have a 4.00 x 18 Dunlop Sports, or a similar Barum, but neither company's product was anything like a modern rider would recognise as a racing design. Rather, they looked like a road bike tyre which was suffering from the cold and had broken out in goose bumps. As a result, drive was always at a premium and riders spent much of their time seeking out lines which gave good grip. Throttle subtlety and feel for the track were two skills that were invaluable – which explains why so many of the good riders were extremely competitive at both trials and scrambles. In this scenario, the four-stroke's instant power and inherently better driving ability was invaluable.

The 490cc engine, which was virtually square in configuration, gave way first to a new long-stroke 498cc motor in 1968 and finally to the slightly more square 84 x 90mm design, which was to eventually become the B.50MX and its road going derivatives.

"Three days later, a huge cardboard box arrived at Warrington Station and what came out was the most beautiful motorcycle I had ever seen."

There are two ways of looking at the B.50. Firstly, its problems: It is fragile, loses its racing edge with frightening rapidity, and has some truly appalling inherent weaknesses. For example, the gearbox and clutch are both grossly under-engineered and all the main castings are far too insubstantial. Further, the engine carries far too light a flywheel for a production engine.

All these features are the result of two things. Firstly, there was a lack of resources at the BSA factory and a shortage of development funds. And what little money there was available was misused.

Second, and of just as much importance, the race shop was interested only in winning Grands Prix. As far as a BSA contracted rider was concerned, the engine had to last for just 90 minutes: two 45-minute races. After that, the motor could be scrapped – and often was. During those races, the works man wanted the minimum weight and the maximum power, and in the B.50 he got both.

Riding a good B.50 is still one of the most exciting experiences in motorcycling. The power is instant, brutal and totally unsophisticated. It arrives like a bomb going off – crude, direct and unbeatable. Even today, the B.50 is competitive against any single- cylinder four-stroke in the world in the 15mph-40mph range, and no, I am not looking at the engine through rose-tinted goggles because I was a BSA man. No engine hits harder or sooner than a crisp B.50.

Good as the B.50 was, my greatest problem was getting one to test. BSA was unused to journalists asking for racing bikes to assess, and probably, had the factory been in a more sound financial position and not so desperate for publicity in the USA, this story would never have been told. Still, after months of pestering, there came a 'phone call from BSA Group advertising manager Ivor Davies, asking which was my nearest British rail station so the factory could dispatch a test B.50 to me.

Three days later, a huge cardboard box arrived at Warrington and, being on good terms with the station staff, we attacked the parcel like kids at Christmas. What came out was then, and still is now, one of the most exciting moments of my motorcycling life, for instead of a standard B.50, with its horrendously ugly white-painted frame and fibre-glass side panels, there appeared the most beautiful motorcycle I had ever seen. The frame was chromed, and the engine, with the fins chopped back and staggered like the works bikes, was stove-enamelled black, with only the points cover and rocker box caps left polished. It was lean, light and the epitome of a racing motorcycle, and it held my heart from that moment on.

The following day was a Saturday and I soon learnt that the B.50 was not nearly so forgiving as the semi-works Bultaco which I normally rode. For a start, the BSA didn't forgive. A carefully worked out run and bump was the only way to coax the high compression, lightly fly-wheeled motor ▸

into life. Then there was its endearing habit of stalling at low revs, and the equally charming trait of lurching across the track in a straight line whenever the power was turned on. Everything about the bike was precise and demanding – as one would expect from a Grand Prix replica.

Just 24 hours later, I rode it at a local scramble and won all three races with an ease that flattered my riding ability. The B.50 was just so quick out of corners it defied belief. Nothing could live with it.

In fact, my BSA was a product of Cyril Halliburn's quality control department. There, engine test shop fitters John Kay and Martin Russell (now owner of Rustler Racing ) developed the BSA speedway engines on a shoe-string budget. It was in this tiny workshop that my works BSA had been born.

John remembers being surprised when he was asked to build the bike but, because of the great fund of goodwill towards motocross in the factory, was delighted to do so.

Martin Russell described the bike as one in a series of "grey" projects done in the quality control workshop – "legal foreigners, which we always enjoyed doing..."

No doubt to the disappointment of many modern day BSA fans, I have to report the engine gave only 33.4bhp at 6,200rpm on the dyno. This compares with the 23bhp or so of a standard motor straight off the production line, and is at something of a variance with the 32bhp the factory claimed for production engines.

I soon grew to love the bike and had a lot of fun on it both in scrambles and also in grass tracks. The B.50 was much faster than a JAP or Jawa off the line, and was a deadly weapon in the tight Saturday night grass tracks, which used to be a feature of the agricultural shows in the north-west of England and mid-Wales. Eventually, the factory asked for the return of their bike and the holiday was over. Well, it should have been.

I had taken care to let BSA works manager Alistair Cave, and also Ivor Davies and Cyril Halliburn know of my enthusiasm for the bike, and so my request to buy the B.50 was favourably received. I cannot be sure, but I think I paid £170 for the BSA as it stood – or so I thought.

Al Cave invited me to bring the bike back to factory for "a check over", and when it returned, the standard frame had been magically transformed into a Reynolds 531 works job and the bike had grown magnesium fork sliders, brake plates and a new top-half, along with the cam used on the speedway engine. If you knew where to look, and you met with the approval of BSA hard-liners, there were still racing bits to be found at Small Heath – despite what the history books will tell you today.

There were good, practical reasons for the generosity of the factory, but the key reason for helping me, and this must never be forgotten, was that the middle management at the BSA loved bikes – and they loved racing, too. They didn't have a works team any more but they did have a young, keen rider who was enamoured of BSAs as much as they were, and who could manage the occasional win to sustain the illusion. As a result, I was treated like the factory's favourite son. Probably they knew the writing was well and truly on the wall and this was going to be their last fling in motocross for a long, long time.

I continued to race the BSA, and perhaps my proudest moment was winning a North-Western Centre grass track outright, and against good opposition, too. And, if proof be needed, that victory alone speaks volumes for how quick is the B.50 even when compared to alcohol-burning engines like JAPs and Jawas.

Every three months, I would take the bike back to BSA and John or Martin would carefully rebuild it and, after showing due courtesy to Al Cave and Cyril, off I would go again. For a centre runner of no great merit, it was heaven on earth. Then the crunch came when the factory was closed forever and clearly, my time as a works rider was over too.

I raced a Cheney BSA the following year, 1974, supported by Eric Cheney himself. The Cheney was a superb bike but I didn't form the same sort of harmonious relationship as I did with the BSA. Silly as it sounds, I loved the BSA because it was so much a part of that tiny sliver of history that was both me and BSA.

So, the BSA sat at the back of the workshop with a blanket over it, and I was suffering at the hands of a wife who wanted the BSA turned into a new three-piece suite – so I sold it. Abraham sacrificing Isaac? These are as nothing compared with my feelings as the BSA disappeared. But all was not lost, for it is here that the God of Simple Scramblers took a hand.

The bike was sold to a chap in Widnes, who wanted a toy for his son. Unfortunately for him, but so very, very luckily for me, the B.50 maintained its history of being impossible to start in the hands of a novice and a swine to ride when it eventually did. So, when I tried to buy the bike back from its new owner six months later, he was openly hostile and accused me of selling him a real donkey – and that is absolutely true. This was to be the bike's, and my, saviour.

Eventually, the son joined the RAF and was posted to Kinloss, in north-east Scotland. Here, some RAF lads tried to ride the bike but with little success, and it was sold to a civilian mechanic on the base. He in turn swopped it with Bob Fraser, chairman of the VMCC in Scotland, and as true a gentleman and motorcycle enthusiast as ever existed.

Bob had a play on the bike and found it to be the most unsuitable trail bike in the universe. His attempts at tracing the bike's origin had proved fruitless, although he always harboured suspicions about its parentage. Enquiries to BSA marque expert Roy Bacon revealed nothing. However, this is no criticism of the arch guru of statistics. Only someone intimately involved with racing BSAs would be able to decipher the engine and frame numbers for what they were, so – thinking he owned an early CCM – Bob entered the bike in Sotheby's auction at the last Classic' Bike Show to be held at Belle Vue in 1986. Reluctantly, he was persuaded to place a very low reserve of £700 on the bike in order to ensure a sale.

So, there was I, wandering around looking at the glittering array of Vincents, Broughs and Manx Nortons waiting to go under the hammer, and to my amazement, and then delight, I saw "my" B.50 looking only slightly the worse for wear, having been painted gold and wearing a pair of plastic mudguards. I nearly wept for joy and, after a moment of hesitation because I was desperately short of money at the time, I hatched a plot to repatriate the bike.

A good friend of mine was Chris Hawley, the owner of Abasport, who imported high quality touring accessories, which he sold at shows. My luck was well and truly in because Chris had a stand at Belle Vue. In an earlier life, Chris had been a successful second-hand car dealer and so was an expert in the auction ring. We held a council of war. First, we decided how much I could afford. Initially, this was £1200 at the absolute maximum – and that would have wiped me out financially since I was in the trough of what is euphemistically known as a 'financially challenging' period . Then I went for a wander round and returned to up the limit to £1500–and remember, these are 1986 prices.

By the time I reached home, I had to 'phone Chris and issue fresh instructions to go to £1750, and by Sunday morning it was up to £2250. I just had to have my BSA back! I still couldn't rest and a 'phone call to my ever-loving mum raised the stakes again; £3,500 was absolutely the end. After this, someone else would have to own my B.50.

We both felt it was best if I stayed well away from the ▸

**1**
**Amal Concentric carburettor is a trick magnesium item.**

**2**
**When I grow up, can I have a mudguard bracket with works holes in it?**

1
AMAL

2

auction and showed no interest in the bike, leaving the clever stuff to Hawley. How I lasted the afternoon out I will never know, but at 4pm Chris casually called to say he had been the only bidder and the BSA had been knocked down to me for £700, plus Sotheby's 10% buyer's premium. That night, before I went to bed, I visited the workshop with tears in my eyes. And if that sounds soppy, I don't care.

In the deal was the original box of spares I had sold with the bike 10 years before, and I must confess to a certain degree of embarrassment when I had to contact Bob regarding these and he began quizzing me about the bike. As any of us would be, he was less than pleased at losing out on what should have been a financial bonanza, but in the true tradition of motorcycle enthusiasts, rather than speculators, he was genuinely pleased that the bike had come back to me rather than ending up in some dealer's stock with Japan or Switzerland as its final destination.

The B.50 hadn't suffered too badly in its sojourn away from home because, as I have noted, of the fact it can't be used for anything but serious racing, and so had done very little work. Personal difficulties prevented me doing anything to the bike during that winter, but the following year I got down to work.

A dear friend of mine was Fred Barlow, who had been BSA's last apprentice working in the competition shop. Fred was the same age as me and we became very close. When BSA folded he set up a business in Tamworth tuning B.50s, and there was no-one better in the world to look after my works bike.

Fred stripped the motor and reported it to be in the same condition as when John Kay last re-built it in 1973. It wasn't race fresh, but since the bike was never going to be used in anger again, Fred simply screwed everything back together carefully and we left it at that.

Meanwhile, I worked on the cycle parts, restoring the bits that were there and replacing those that had been damaged over the years. The aim was not to achieve a concours restoration because the bike was never in this state after the first lap of its life. Rather, I aimed to replicate the bike as it would have been at the start of the 1973 season; clean and tidy and ready to race. Purists might be offended with this strategy but even in retirement the B.50 was a racing bike–not some ornament to be polished.

And, as with all good fairy stories, there was a happy ending. I took the B.50 to the BSA Owners' North-Eastern Rally so I could share it with other enthusiasts. After the judging, I cracked the B.50 up and gave it a quick burst round the show ring, just like the Saturday night grass tracks we both used to love so much. As the staccato bark bounced off the judging tents and hot-dog vans I became misty eyed and very grateful I had raced this bike when we were both in our prime.

One could never accuse the bike of being civilised, but that evocative sound must have done something for the judges too for they gave the B.50 the best competition bike award, which made us both very happy. Clutching that pewter tankard took us both back many years, and if I was not mistaken, I'm sure I saw that aggressive staggered fin engine nod in approval as I went up to receive the trophy on our behalf. But, of course, that would only happen in a fairy story, wouldn't it?

**1**
**Melling remains the same liberal hippy that he was aged 20.**

**2**
**Bronze welded Reynolds 531 frame - a real works job.**

**3**
**Melling's bike had magnesium fork sliders and lightweight hubs machined as a foreigner in the BSA tool room.**

So, that should have been the end of the story. The book should have been closed. There would have been a little bit of a tuck in with the little one's blanket, a goodnight kiss, the final "night, night" and the lights switched off.

But not for this bike…

I found a new love and the BSA wasn't part of her life – although she knew the bike was incredibly special for me. Although Carol had never been to a motorcycle race before she met me, my lovely new bride took to racing as if she had been born in the paddock.

I found an original Cheney B.50 BSA, just like the one I had ridden when I had been sponsored by Eric. Fred Barlow prepared the engine and I won the National Vintage Grass Track Championship in 1994 with Carol supporting me all the way and our baby daughter travelling to every round with us. It was a truly wonderful time and represented everything that was good in my new life.

Now for our family, B.50s meant the Cheney. The works BSA sat in the back of the workshop, once more under a dust cover and if not neglected, no longer in the limelight as it once was. But the bike was warm, dry and happy and could have still been there today except for one of the great tragedies in the history of the British motorcycle industry. On Tuesday, September 16, 2003, there was an immense of amount of damage done to the National Motorcycle Museum by a single, recklessly discarded cigarette end, which started a fire in a pile of cardboard boxes and air filters. The fire took hold in seconds, and eventually it took 120 firefighters to bring it under control. Three hundred and eighty of the world's finest classic British bikes were either destroyed or very badly damaged.

The whole classic motorcycling world was in shock, and everyone who loved British bikes was determined to help in whatever way they could.

It wasn't only the huge amount of damage that had been done and, thanks to the near miraculous efforts of the museum's staff and friends many of the bikes could be, and were, restored. A secondary issue was that even the most brilliant restoration is just that – something that is changed from the original.

Some months after the fire, I received a phone call from Roy Richards, the museum's inspirational founder. I liked Roy a lot – an awful lot – for his vision, his commitment and his belief in gathering Britain's motorcycle heritage on one site and preserving it for future generations.

Roy knew of my bike and wanted it because the machine was original. Our BSA was just as it finished its racing career.

We had a family meeting. My daughter was involved in the discussion because she was old enough to understand what was happening. Her view was one that we all felt. She said: "It's a great bike, dad, but I've never seen you race it or even heard it run.

"If it was my Cheney (she always viewed the Cheney as her personal pet!) I would go mad, but the BSA is just another nice bike."

Carol was a little gentler but voiced more or less the same opinion. There was also a sub-text which was left unspoken. The BSA belonged to a different life – a life that was my life and not that of my family in 2003. All the wonderful memories of John Kay, Martin Russell, Cyril Halliburn and Small Heath were mine – not ours.

So, it took very little persuasion to let the BSA go to where it should be – the National Motorcycle Museum – to be seen and enjoyed by the 250,000 visitors the museum has each year.

It's also right and proper that the bike should continue to be a star as the last works BSA ever produced, and ridden by the worst factory rider ever supported by BSA. ◆

①

②

③

# Hesketh Venom

The gentleman's motorcycling carriage

THERE'S a much quoted adage from the yacht racing world. It comes in the form of a question. Here we go: "How do you make a small fortune from racing an ocean-going yacht?"

Answer: "Start with a big one!"

If the adage applies to super yachts it is even more apposite for a privately funded Formula 1 car-racing team.

Then, if you really want to up your game, become a motorcycle manufacturer when you have absolutely zero expertise or prior experience. Now, you really can whizz through some serious piles of cash.

Yet this is just what Thomas Alexander Fermor-Hesketh, the Third Baron Hesketh, managed to do – and with some considerable aplomb.

At four years of age, Lord Hesketh inherited 3300 acres of Northamptonshire countryside; the 18th century Baroque, Easton Neston House; Towcester racecourse; and ample space to slaughter lots of tame pheasants and partridges in an idyllic English country setting. There were also five lodges, three farms and the entire village of Hulcote.

After briefly working for a super posh firm of stockbrokers in San Francisco, Lord Hesketh returned to Easton Neston to manage the family estate. In this respect, he had a refreshingly novel approach to money: spend as much as you reasonably, or unreasonably, can – and as fast as possible.

In 1972, he established Hesketh Racing, which was run by a suitably polished ex-racing driver, and second-hand car dealer, called Anthony 'Bubbles' Horsley. Two years later they were in Formula 1. The team made its first F1 appearance at the 1973 Monaco Grand Prix. In typical Hesketh Racing style, they arrived in the harbour via the lord's yacht.

There was a Bell Jet Ranger helicopter to avoid the queues of anorak-clad, peaked- hat wearing, banner-waving oiks waiting to get into race meetings, and a pinstriped Rolls Royce as a pit car – much classier than the vans that lesser teams used.

Lord Hesketh felt that accepting sponsorship was vulgar, and somewhat unsporting, so he financed the whole £400,000 racing project – give or take, around £3.5million in today's money – entirely from his own personal wealth. Although far less than other F1 teams' budgets this was still a lot of money. However, by late-1975 even the very wealthy Lord Hesketh was beginning to feel the pinch and so wound up the team.

Next, the noble lord was about to learn three very important, and inter-related, lessons. ▸

**Above**
**The Hesketh has the appearance of a very high quality, home built special.**

**Right**
**Hesketh four-valve twin is huge and very heavy.**

The first is one I know all too well from the days when I owned and ran Europe's biggest motorcycle event: people will take any amount of anything for free, but it's a different matter if they have to spend some of their own money. So, as long as the free champers and canapés flowed then the queue of best mates – do the aristocracy have 'mates' except as a breeding stock? – stretched all the way down the Easton Neston drive.

Things were different when, despite all of Hesketh's uber-wealthy contacts, he wanted money for his new project: an English Super Grand Tourer (ESGT) motorcycle in the style of a Brough Superior or Vincent. So, from day one the exercise was underfunded.

The second lesson was the obverse side of the first coin. Lots of rich, sophisticated people would have had a Hesketh free of charge, but it was a very different story when it came to getting those same wealthy people to part with their money.

Even if the customers had been there to actually buy the new bike, the proposed 5000 units for the first year was an impossibly lofty goal – even for an established manufacturer.

At launch, the Hesketh was a walloping third more expensive than the truly upmarket king of the SGTs – the BMW R100RS, a bike that really was ridden by merchant bankers and aristos, as well as people like me.

The final lesson was perhaps the hardest of all. Production engineering is nothing, but nothing, like making tiny numbers of prototypes – F1 style.

The project was reportedly touted around City of London investors, based on 5000 units a year, and this figure needs considering. It's a good number in terms of amortising production costs, but it's also fantasy land high for a start up project. Based on a 49-week production year, 5000 units represents 102 bikes every week – 14-plus a day. That's seven before lunch break and seven afterwards, all heading relentlessly for the delivery bay – day after day, and week after week.

To make this number of motorcycles, or anything else for that matter, you need a real stock control system. A purchasing manager chasing down every penny of production costs; homologation engineers to ensure compliance and actual staff to look after all the non-glamorous, but utterly essential, minutiae of running a factory, from having the photocopier serviced to ordering the cleaning materials for the toilets. All of this is a galaxy away from the freewheeling, 'can do', atmosphere of race, or prototype, engineering.

The initial idea for the ESGT allegedly came from Harvey Postlethwaite, who designed the Hesketh F1 cars. Mr Postlethwaite was a bike fan and thought there was a vacant slot in the market for a true English Super Grand Tourer, laden with top spec equipment and covered with inch-deep layers of nostalgia.

With the ghosts of Vincent and Brough Superior – and it's worth noting both of these luxury brands failed – hovering over the workshop at Easton Neston, the bike had to be a traditional British V-Twin. The problem was no-one at Hesketh could design one so the job was put out to unofficial tender, and the well-established British Weslake company, down in Rye, on the south coast of England, got the contract.

Weslake was highly respected in the car racing world, having built a very successful V12, and they also had experi-

**Below**
**The Hesketh was conceived to be a thoroughbred stallion – but unfortunately it turned out to be a not very well bred one.**

**Right**
**The gentleman's carriage.**

"As the most expensive production bike on the market there should have been attention to the finest detail – but there wasn't."

ence of motorcycle manufacturing. In 1968, they made a 490cc big-bore conversion kit for the BSA 440cc, B.44 motocrosser, and then later a 500cc, four-valve speedway engine, which carried Peter Collins to the 1976 World title.

The Weslake speedway engine was designed by Ron Valentine, and he came up with a rather clever 1000cc v-twin which used two, four-valve, 500cc speedway engines on a common crankcase. Clearly, if you intended to make a 1000cc, four-valve ESGT you would go to someone who had already proved they could do the job: except that Weslake hadn't!

The Weslake engines were all race motors and, whatever other manifold weaknesses racers have both intellectually and emotionally, we are good with engines. We know about careful, pre-race warming, and we know about maintenance and meticulous oil changes, too. Road engines, and their users, are very different.

A road rider might hammer the man bits off a bike, potter round the country lanes at 50mph, or nip down into town on a blisteringly hot summer's day when the traffic barely moves. A road bike engine has to do all these jobs without going bang.

I think a further problem was that the original Weslake V-Twin was designed to run on alcohol and this keeps engines very cool. By contrast, the Hesketh engine used standard pump fuel and was expected to perform well in a very wide range of conditions: it didn't.

From the outset, the motor did not make good power, the rear cylinder ran hot and the porous crankcases leaked copious amount of oil. Then things got worse...

As an SGT, the new Hesketh was designed to have shaft drive – a la BMW. Why wouldn't it? The answer was BMW had already threatened to sue the rice bowls and chopsticks off Yamaha, for patent infringement, when they had tried to use a shaft drive system suspiciously like that emanating from Bavaria. Hesketh intended to use the same design as Yamaha but, wholly sensibly, took fright.

The fix wasn't really a solution at all. The gearbox was converted to chain drive and proved to be a clonky, imprecise affair.

The chassis was good. If there was one area of expertise where Britain still ruled the world in 1980 it was making bikes which handled and steered, and the bronze- welded, Reynolds 531 frame – bright nickel-plated in the best tradition – worked well.

Top quality, state-of-the-art Marzocchi suspension and equally high-quality Brembo brakes made the best use of the chassis.

Not that everything was rosy. The V1000 was a truly enormous lump of motorcycle. The bike has a near 60in (1524mm) wheelbase and the seat height is 32in (81cm). This is a fine configuration for an experienced adult, male rider cruising down to the casino in Monte Carlo. However, forget it if you are under 5ft 10in (1.8m), or – Heaven forbid – a woman. Indulging in stop-start riding is a seriously tricky activity.

At 550lb (220kg) the V1000 isn't a bike for dragging around car parks either. This is an SGT and needs to live exclusively on the open road.

As the most expensive production bike on the market there should have been attention to the finest detail – but there wasn't. The instrument cluster looked very downmarket and this was a constant reminder to owners that although the Hesketh talked well, it wasn't quite there.

The first time I saw the bike in the flesh was at the Birmingham Bike Show. The whole Hesketh stand was roped off and access was via a big, tough-looking security guy. Either you had an invitation and were permitted entry, or you presented your business card and hoped for the best. Behind the velvet, Lord Hesketh smiled and entertained while the delicate, botoxed beautiful people smiled, chatted, drank freely of the complimentary champagne – and glanced bemusedly, not to say somewhat nervously, at the leather-jacketed lower classes looking in from the other side of the barriers. ▸

①

②

③

"Behind the velvet, Lord Hesketh smiled and entertained while the delicate, bo-toxed beautiful people smiled, chatted and drank freely of the complimentary champagne."

After 20 minutes, I gave up and went on to the completely open, and very welcoming, Honda stand to admire their new GL1100 Goldwing, which really was a high-speed, gentleman's SGT.

At launch, the media greeted the new Hesketh with extremely restrained enthusiasm. British moto-journos faced a huge emotional problem. Triumph was effectively dead, as was Norton, and so we desperately wanted a new flag carrier for the Union Jack. Sadly, Hesketh wasn't to be the answer.

I never rode a Hesketh at the start of its life but I did so about five years later. An upmarket car dealer I knew had taken one in part exchange against a Ferrari convertible and wanted my help to sell it. I had a go on it and the bike was exactly in keeping with its reputation: underpowered compared with the Japanese opposition and with a crude, old-fashioned feel about it.

But back to the story. The prototypes were produced in Lord Hesketh's stable and a key player was development engineer Mick Broome. This is what he said in an interview with Visordown website: "We were based in the stable block on his (Lord Hesketh's) estate. I was employed as development engineer and we steadily lurched on from disaster to disaster from then on. The Hesketh was going to be the superbike of its time, so we chose a big V-Twin as it mirrored the Vincents and Brough Superiors.

"It took about three months to put the first bike together, but the design was already done beforehand. We launched the bike in 1980, outside the big house. Mike Hailwood was there, along with all the world's press. They loved the bike and thought it was what the country needed, but the fact was we launched it so we could find someone to invest in the project. We didn't have the manufacturing skills, only the design ones. But no one came out of the woodwork to back us.

"Then the City launched its venture capital scheme and was looking for companies to back. They gave Lord Hesketh the backing.

"When the factory closed we set up a company to look after the customers who had already purchased their bike."

After the first few bikes, production was moved to a new factory in nearby Daventry, where the big USP was an all-new CNC workstation capable of producing very high quality machining. This was absolutely state of the art for 1982. Unfortunately, the rest of works was far behind and, in particular, the quality of castings for the new engine was dreadful.

Eventually, a total of around 250 V1000s trickled out of the two assembly areas.

The money evaporated with nothing to show for the expenditure and, despite various attempts to keep the V1000 alive, it fell to Mick Broome to look after the machines which had been made and to incorporate what are called the EN10 modifications. These effectively cured the leaking crankcases and made the gearbox useable. This brings us to our test bike.

This V1000 was thoroughly sorted out before owner Ron Willis bought it. Ron said: "I always fancied a Hesketh, but I wanted one which had everything done to it. This bike fitted the bill perfectly."

First impressions are always interesting and mine are now very much influenced by the current mass of retro bikes on sale: this is a fascinating quirk of fate. Where, originally, the Hesketh looked dull and old fashioned compared with the opposition, now it appears to be right on message. It's easy to look at the V1000 through only a slightly rose-tinted visor and think that some new, niche manufacturer has produced the bike.

There is no doubt Ron's Hesketh really has been sorted. All air-cooled big twins sort of wheeze into life and this is what

4

**1**
**Aristocratic name and logo was supposed to produce the most desirable motorcycle in the world - it didn't.**

**2**
**The V1000's instruments were just one example of ancillary fittings which were anything but premium.**

**3**
**A well-sorted Hesketh really gets on with the job in true, English, Grand Tourer style.**

**4**
**The Hesketh is tall, long and heavy and only works on the open road.**

the Hesketh does. Originally, the cacophony that emanated from the engine was truly off-putting but on the fettled Hesketh it's all rather interesting and quirky.

What isn't any different is the height of the bike. I'm 5ft 11in (1.85m) in riding boots and I was just about comfortable wriggling the bike round in Ron's drive.

However, there is an interesting shift in perception regarding the bike's weight. Thirty-seven years ago, 550lbs (250kgs) was a seriously porky bike: now it isn't. In fact, finding anything other than a track day focused sports bike which is sub 400lbs (181kgs) is difficult. Triumph's Thruxton R, which prides itself on svelte proportions, tips the scales at 446lbs (201kgs), so the Hesketh is no longer enormously portly.

From the outset, it becomes apparent the gearbox works fine. It's not feather light and laser accurate but, by applying a bit of thought, I never missed a gear during my ride so it is clearly functional.

The power too is very interesting. The Weslake engine was touted as giving 82hp at a mere 6800rpm and 78lb-ft of torque at 1000rpm less. Probably, none of the original motors produced these figures in real life because they ran so hot, but Ron's Hesketh does make better power than a good 850 Norton Commando and so, in the real world, the riding experience is very pleasant.

On the fast, English country lanes that formed our test run, the bike burbled along very satisfactorily in the 65mph range, and on a short stretch of dual carriageway another 10mph was instantly available.

Best of all, it was just the sort of vintagey, Vincenty, Brough Superiory power that the Hesketh team had promised all along.

The big chassis also suits the bike. With modern tyres, the ride really was very pleasant as I ambled down the Hampshire country lanes looking for a peasant or two, to thrash with the riding crop I had tucked in my boots. If the Hesketh had been on sale in 1780, rather than 1980, I feel sure that it would have been the hot ticket as a gentleman's carriage.

Everything works really quite well. There are acres of space for the pilot, and the Memsaab too should she deign to ride pillion. The brakes are not up to modern standards, but who would make a hurried stop on a conveyance of the Hesketh's status: to do so would be thoroughly undignified.

In short, I really enjoyed the whole experience.

It's not only me who thinks this – there is now a growing interest in becoming a member of the 'Heskethisti'. Ten years ago, a V1000 was just a quirky motorcycling anachronism, and prices reflected this. At Bonhams' 2011 October sale a fully sorted V1000, with 4197 miles showing on the odometer, sold for £6,325, including buyers' premium.

Compare this to the £11,000 that the We Sell Classic Bikes dealership received for their V1000 just a few years later. Equally, when some owners are talking about values in excess of £20,000 these are clearly aspirational rather than achievable.

Much as a Hesketh is a nice thing to ride there are a lot of other really desirable motorcycles available for £10,000 or £12,000. One could choose from a mint MkIII Norton Commando – and still have cash spare – or maybe a Mk 1 Moto Guzzi Le Mans or a BMW R90S. None of these will carry the Hesketh heritage – but they are all better bikes.

As Lord Hesketh first noted in 1978, there is always a price to pay for exclusivity.

The good news is these bikes can be used today, in a practical sense, and there is an enthusiastic owners' club at: http://www.heskethownersclub.org.uk

Many thanks to Ron for letting me join, ever so briefly, the upper classes. ◆

arc
www.arc.be
MELKA
MELKA
HONDA
NGK
SPARK PLUGS
RON HASLAM
2
METZELER
MOTORRAD-REIFEN
CB 1100
R

# CB1100R

Big, powerful and very successful

Above all else, I love honesty in a motorcycle – and everything else too, for that matter. If a bike is a real dog – and I'm thinking of things like AMC's post-war James and Francis Barnett products – then, in a perverse sort of way, I'm happy with this.

The same goes for marketing disasters like the cataclysmically bad Ariel 3 or the Suzuki RE5 Wankel, the bike which almost single-handedly destroyed the Japanese company.

At the other end of the scale, no right-thinking person could not fall in love with a BSA DBD 34 Gold Star – one of those bikes that looks as if it is doing 100mph sitting on its centre stand.

And, of course, the purist of the pure are race bikes – thoroughbreds built for speed and carrying no mixed messages or civilising ambiguities.

For all these reasons, the CB1100R is a real conundrum. You know, from reputation, just how successful the bike was and yet the enormous thing sat in the paddock just can't possibly be a race bike, can it?

The answer is yes – and very much so.

The first thing that strikes everyone is the bike's size. Parked up in the paddock, the Honda is not your lithe, toned sprinter waiting to trot out and compete in the 200m. It's more a rugby prop forward, warming up ready for a head-crunching, 80 minutes of pitched battle.

Yet, look at the same prop forward and you will see both plenty of scar tissue and a shirt stretched tight by bulging muscle. The odd lump of ear might be missing but this is no couch potato wobbling out on to the field. Note the magnesium clutch and alternator covers, and listen to the tenor wail of the 1062cc engine, and it becomes readily apparent that, beneath the corrosion, scrapes and immense size there lurks a real racing motorcycle.

The CB1100R is one of a number of bikes Honda has produced over the years to circumvent homologation rules for racing. Series organisers will demand that a certain number of examples of a particular machine must be produced in order to comply with their regulations. For example, World Superbike is run with machines based, very loosely, on production motorcycles which the ordinary customer can – in theory at least – walk into a showroom and buy.

Manufacturers ruthlessly exploit and bend the regulations right up to breaking point, and so there have been some extremely interesting motorcycles sold over the years as "homologation specials". The CB1100R is one of the best since it took the rule book right to the edge of legality and then, initially at least, fell over the regulatory cliff.

Take yourself back to 1980, when Grand Prix racing was still ruled by 500cc two-strokes. These were pure race bikes and were a million miles away from anything in mass production. Both Yamaha and Suzuki had attempts at bringing the GP world to the road rider with four-cylinder two-strokes but the truth was the ordinary motorcyclist on the street wanted a big, four-cylinder four-stroke.

The next bit of history is that one of the most prestigious one-off races in the world in the 1970s and '80s was the Castrol Six-Hour race, held at Amaroo in Australia. In terms of an advertising event to promote Asian sales, this event ran a close second to the Suzuka Eight-Hour race, which spawned some equally exotic machinery.

Honda was determined to win this race, and so took their CB900F road bike and gave it a full race make-over. The CB1100R was to be no 'tweaked-up' road machine but, as far rules could be stretched, a full-blown race bike. ▸

**1**
**CB1100R is a proper race bike – despite being road legal..**

**2**
**Melling eases the big Honda out of the chicane. This is not a bike to be thrown about!**

**3**
**You don't often see a speedometer on a serious race bike.**

**4**
**The CB1100R's engine is a big, traditional four-cylinder Japanese design.**

"The CB900 lump was bored to 70mm, resulting in a whopping capacity of 1062cc."

2
452
Shell
HONDA
HONDA
MOCHECK
METZELER
RON HASLAM
FERODO
❷

❸
OIL
NEUTRAL
HIGH BEAM
TURN
TURN

HONDA
ECK
REGINA CHAIN
RON HASLAM
CB 110
R
❹

452
2
METZELER
Shell
HONDA
MOCHECK
FERODO
❶

MELKA
MELKA
METZELER
Shell
HONDA
MOCHECK
2
HONDA
NGK SPARK PLUGS
REGINA CHAIN
RON HASLAM
CB 1100
R
❷

The first job was to lighten and stiffen the CB900F frame. This was done by increasing the quality of the tubing and by making the frame in one piece, instead of having the right-hand frame down tube removable to help with servicing. Even so, with a wheelbase of 1475mm (58in in real money), and a saddle height of 805mm (31in), this is no Moto Martin or Harris race frame.

The engine received even more treatment. The CB900 lump was bored to 70mm, resulting in a whopping capacity of 1062cc. A race camshaft was put into the engine, along with forged pistons, which increased the compression ratio to an eye-watering 10:1. This high-compression ratio has proved to be a consistent wrecker of the starter motor clutch rings over the years, on bikes used on the road. A close ratio transmission went into the gearbox and the drive was protected with a wider primary chain and lighter clutch.

What could be seen was, in some ways, even more sensational than what was hidden. The road bike's high 'bars were retained, but a huge bikini fairing wrapped itself round the cockpit area. Behind the fairing was an equally mammoth six-gallon, alloy fuel tank, and the world's most comfortable race seat ensured the pilot was going nowhere as he wrestled the big Honda round the race tracks. Ultra-lightweight magnesium, painted with traditional gold paint to reduce corrosion, was used for the clutch and alternator covers.

The chassis was still very much late-'70s with a traditional, twin-shock rear end and steel swinging arm, although the forks did have air assistance in lieu of anti-dive.

The reality of the situation was a race bike that weighed in at an incredible 563lbs (256kg) – more than twice as heavy as its Grand Prix cousins. At the other end of the scale, the 1062cc engine produced a walloping 115bhp at 9,000rpm – not that far behind the GP thoroughbreds.

Honda UK, one of Honda's key importers in the world, was sceptical about the bike and ordered just 100 units with deliveries starting in November 1980. The idea was the bike would be used for the Honda UK race effort, private race teams running Hondas and a few, very wealthy, private Honda enthusiasts.

There were two big problems with the new bike. First, it took the phrase 'sports focused' to an all new level of accuracy. In fact, sports focused was actually well wide of the mark. 'Race track focused' was actually the truth.

The second issue was the price. The CB1100R sold for £3,700, which was actually one of the great bargains of all time. The snag was that Honda's own, and very fine, CB900F had a price sticker of £1,999 and for a much better road bike.

The final issue was the world was a very different place in 1980. The idea of paying a lot of money for a race bike you would never use in anger would have seemed strange – and the idea of 'collectors' editions' of things was still in its newly born infancy.

In summary, the CB1100R was a true classic dinosaur – big, brutal and, by the standards of the day, monstrously powerful. The price, and the shortage of collector buyers, meant only 4050 CB1100Rs were produced over three years – but what a three-year period the bike was going to have.

The fact I was able to ride the bike at all was thanks to the efforts of Peter Spowage and Clive Brooker – at the time, the driving forces behind the Historic Endurance Racing Team. Because of the enthusiasm of Clive and Peter, some of the wonderful, old, long-distance race bikes from the 1960s, 70s and early 80s were seen in action at events all over Europe.

The CB1100R that I rode was the genuine, ex-Ron Haslam bike on which he won the MCN Street Bike series in 1981 and 1982. At the time, it was owned by a secretive enthusiast who allowed the Historic Endurance Racing Team to demonstrate the bike on occasions – provided his anonymity was protected.

One of the events on the team's tour was the Bikers' Classics festival held at Spa-Francorchamps in Belgium. Although heavily spiced up with bells and whistles, thanks to ex-world champions and mouth-watering GP bikes, the event is essentially a giant, three-day track bash for classic race bikes. Legally, it is not racing – but it would take an expert eye to split the difference.

As I lined up with a host of late classic race bikes, it soon became clear the CBR was going to be the centre of attention. With Ron Haslam's name emblazoned on the fairing, I faced a stream of autograph hunters and, except for being taller, fatter, having a lot less hair and about 1% of Rocket Ron's riding ability, I might well have got away with the deception but, with the odds stacked against me, I didn't even try.

Out on the track, it becomes clear the CB is carrying its age well – despite being unrestored. The 115 horses allowed us to run with the faster Triumph triples and, once the glazing had been scrubbed off the pads, the Honda discs were well up to hauling down the 600 plus pounds (272kgs) of heavy metal which made up the fully fuelled Honda.

Down the straights, and on braking too, the CB1100R can run with the hot classics without too much trouble. The problems begin on the corners. This needs explaining. A decent BSA/Triumph triple pushes out well over 90bhp and weighs around 340lbs (154kgs). This means the Honda is carrying almost the weight of a pillion passenger, plus a full set of touring luggage more than a pure classic race machine. ▸

**1**
**The Honda was at its best on sweeping, 100mph-plus bends.**

**2**
**There's enough room for a birthday party behind the Honda's immense fairing.**

**3**
**Trick bits are everywhere on the CB from the huge, six-gallon alloy fuel tank to the magnesium engine cases.**

3

Running modern race Avons, the triples go round corners like 125 GP bikes and also get their power on extremely early. By contrast, the Honda carries Metzeler road tyres and it was the team's policy to run these at very low pressures. Apparently, Honda Britain ran 39psi in the front tyres in contrast to the 27psi that were in the Metzelers when I rode the bike. The result is although the Honda is wonderfully planted on long corners it is reluctant to change direction. This is where the classic race bikes do their disappearing act.

Still, none of this matters much compared with the delight of riding such a thoroughbred machine. The gearshift is in the perfect position, being on the right with up for down. Until anyone has ridden a machine with this configuration, it will never be apparent what a con trick the Japanese worked on us with a left-hand change running the wrong way. The change is sweet, light and bullet proof, and the motor not at all cammy. Simply wind on the big four and it goes faster and faster – with 135mph popping up on the speedo a couple of times a lap.

At 5ft 11in, I am too tall for a road racer so I love the vast amount of space in the cockpit and behind the fairing. The handling is impeccable, the brakes excellent. This is a bike I really could fancy taking home with me. It is both charismatic and, taken in context, flawless. Carrying a set of sticky Avons or Bridgestones, many modern Superbikes would be given a seriously good run for their money by this veteran Honda.

Today, the CB1100R still remains a little bit of an anachronism. Although not as well-known as the RC30 and RC45 homologation Hondas that followed it, the CB1100R deserves the same iconic status as the later machines. In fact, maybe it should be at the very top of the tree simply because it is the last in the line of big, heavy, pugilist race bikes that any of the major manufacturers produced. It also earns its status because it was a runaway success.

The big bruiser did its job by winning the Castrol Six-Hour race at its first attempt in 1980, with future world champion Wayne Gardner in the saddle.

The following year, the bike was banned for not having a dual seat – banning winners was a common feature of the Castrol Six Hour races – but, in 1982, Honda came back with Gardner again. Wayne's bike was the CB1100RC which had a removable hump to reveal pillion carrying capacity. The bike is still on show in Australia, having never been run since its victory.

In Britain, Ron Haslam won both the 1981 and 1982 MCN Streetbike series, and the bike was just as successful wherever it was raced throughout the world.

With a CV like this, the bike deserves to be an icon. ◆

**In Ron Haslam's hands, the CB1100R won everything in sight**

"The CB is a bike I really could fancy taking home with me."

METZELER
Shell
HONDA
MOCHECK
2
NGK
REGINA
FERODO

Arai
16
RENOLD
DUNLOP
NATIONAL
MOTORCYCLE
MUSEUM
750
67
CHAMPION
AMAL

# 'Slippery Sam'

## The most famous production racer of all time

TO UNDERSTAND the fame accrued by what, in the final analysis, is only a modified street motorcycle it is important to remember just how important production racing was in the late-1960s and early-1970s.

At the same time as enthusiasm for racing road bikes was at its peak, interest in mainstream GPs was at an all-time low ebb, with spectators becoming weary of the endless stream of twin-cylinder Yamaha two-strokes in the smaller classes and the legendary Giacomo Agostini giving high-speed demonstrations with the bigger MVs. By contrast, production racing had a plethora of factory-entered bikes of all sizes, shapes and capacities.

Production racing also offered a huge publicity return for every pound invested. The top bikes were very cheap to make and the leading riders were highly affordable. For example, following Malcolm Uphill's 100mph TT win in 1969, he received £50 prize money and £70 in trade bonuses. This was around a month's wages for a skilled worker of the period, or about £2,000 in current terms.

Compare this with the £1million a month, plus bonuses, which goes into Mr Marquez's bank balance!

However, Malcolm did get to keep the bike on which he had won the TT – which meant an awful lot to him!

Malcolm was later invited to the factory for a VIP reception to celebrate the win. At this star-studded event, the TT winner was publicly thanked – and then given a £12 transistor radio. I bet Marquez has never got one of those from Honda!

The bikes which won were cheap, too. All Triumph racing machines started life as production line rejects. Les Williams, the mechanical genius behind much of Triumph's race success, remembers how the Triumph Tridents for the 1970 TT arrived in the experimental department.

"When a bike was run on the rolling road, if it wasn't up to standard we would get it instead of it being rectified. Our

**1**
**Always an iconic sight**

**2**
**TT fairing is huge and very comfortable at high speeds.**

**3**
**Free revving three cylinder engine has the traditional right-hand gear change with up for first.**

first bikes all had oil pump failures so the main parts of the bikes were fine."

The 1969 Production TT had been a bonanza for Triumph in terms of publicity, with Uphill's 100mph lap becoming the stuff of legends. However, the story nearly had a very different ending. Here's Les again: "When we stripped the bikes down we saw how close we had been to a disaster. The pistons on Malcolm's bike were cracked and they wouldn't have lasted another half lap. Everyone knew then that we needed the triple if we were to carry on winning in production racing."

Not that things were straightforward. Les explains. "The Americans were pressing the BSA board (Triumph were part of the BSA Group) to go to Daytona for 1970 so a decision was made that we were going to race the triple.

"Doug Hele (Triumph's development engineer and the mastermind behind their racing success) came down to the experimental department and explained what we had to do. To be honest it was all a bit of rush. ▸

"The experimental department was a very close team – more like a family than a factory. All the four mechanics were involved in the discussions because although Doug was in overall charge, and I was the foreman or something approximately like this, we were a team and everyone was encouraged to contribute ideas.

"We took a standard triple to Castle Combe, with Percy Tait (Triumph's leading test rider and a very fine racer), and it didn't handle well enough to race seriously so I worked with Rob North, who we already knew from a frame he made for Percy a year earlier, to make a proper race chassis which was the first High Boy frame – and this did handle.

"Rob made the frame in 30 hours from scratch which was an amazing piece of fabrication.

"At the same time, we worked on the standard road engine and we found that it would give plenty of power.

"To prepare for Daytona, in the winter of 1970, we went to South Africa with Ray Pickerell, Paul Smart and a couple of mechanics to get some idea of how the bikes would work in a hot climate, and then it was almost straight to Daytona, which was the most important race of the year in America.

"The production racers had to take very much a back seat until things settled down."

I pressed Les about the importance of the production bikes and his answer was very interesting. "They were just another job. Every job was important and we wanted to win every race we entered but you have to remember that we didn't have a dedicated race shop. Race bikes were done in the experimental department, and always on a very tight budget, so we did what we could with the resources we had."

The Trident production racers were helped hugely by the factory's experience with the Bonnevilles. The alloy fuel tank, rear set footrests and 'Clubman' handlebars were all direct lifts from the twins and, in theory at least, they were all available to be bought as Triumph accessories – as was the brand-new, five-speed, Quaife race gearbox. However, what went into the engine wasn't!

The triples could be made to produce power, and reliably too, in a way the Bonnevilles could never achieve. From a typical figure of 58hp produced by a good Trident road bike, the Triumph team was soon getting 70+ hp of useable power from the production racing engine – equating to a genuine 150mph in the Isle of Man.

Because the triple owed so much of its engineering to the earlier twins, a considerable amount of this racing experience was carried across to the new engine. The TH6 race cam was used, along with ball-ended tappets and W&S valve springs with titanium valve caps and collets. The rockers were lightened and polished for reliability. To help breathing, the cylinder heads were meticulously ported and the high-compression pistons matched to individually machined squish bands in the cylinder heads.

Doug Hele and Williams shared a common passion for the complete racing bike, where neither power nor handling was allowed to take precedence over making a bike that was useable over the whole course of a race.

Les said: "It wasn't the absolute power we wanted but race winning power, which the rider could make the best use of: that was the only thing which counted."

The production racers ran on 27mm, Amal concentric carburettors from the road bikes to comply with regulations.

The Ray Gun silencers, which were loathed by customers on the Trident and Rocket 3 road bikes, were actually a sound piece of engineering. Les tried them without any baffles but found that they were much more efficient with the production, road-legal, reverse flow baffles. It's just a shame they are so ugly! To complement the silencers, the exhaust pipes were raised and tucked in.

**1**
**Slippery Sam at the Bol d'Or.**

**2**
**Slippery Sam at the 1975, ten lap, Production TT which it won with Dave Croxford and Alex George riding and Les Williams the mechanical genius who made the bike so fast and reliable.**

**3**
**Plenty of concentration Melling! That's an irreplaceable piece of motorcycling history that you're riding...**

The standard Trident frame was designed by Doug Hele, and so it was no surprise that the core handling was fine. The biggest improvement was fitting an enormous 250mm double-sided, twin-leading shoe Fontana brake, which was needed to stop the big, heavy triple from 150mph.

The front forks were tweaked by removing the cast shuttle valve damper and replacing this with shuttle valves machined in the Triumph tool room. With the hand-made valves, adjustments of 10 thousandths of an inch could be made and the front forks were then excellent.

Girling built unique dampers for Triumph. They looked like the items you could buy over the counter, but had special damping in them. Girling provided three sets for each bike, all with slightly different damping.

Dunlop supplied the new TT100 supersports road tyres in a 19in size and these larger rims gave a little more ground clearance than the 18in wheels used on many race bikes of the time.

Favoured Triumph dealers could buy most of the special parts used on the works bikes directly from the factory because these had to be at least nominally available to comply with production racing regulations. However, the full tuning kits were very tightly controlled and released only to dealers

③

who were likely to be successful with the bikes they built.

The TT was the biggest production race of the year, and Les set off in June 1970 with high hopes for the race. You can imagine the scene. All the Triumph workers stream out on to the lawns outside the Meriden factory and there is a huge send off. Managing director Lionel Jofeh comes across from Small Heath to shake the team members' hands and wish them Bon Voyage. Except that it wasn't quite like that…

Here's Les. "For a start, we only had one knackered, old Transit van, which belonged to the experimental department. Van hire had just started in Coventry – so we went to Batleys and hired a second Transit. We all piled into the two transits – the whole team.

"I used to watch every penny to save money. I was always worried about management thinking that we were spending too much money on racing, so I had to be careful.

"We all stayed in a little guest house in Douglas. Sometimes, five of us shared one bedroom. It wasn't very posh but we had a nice breakfast – the full English – and then meat and two veg in the evening, so it was good.

"The BSA lot had a real budget and stayed in the Douglas Bay Hotel, but we weren't bothered because we knew we could beat them, so we were happy where we were.

"Norton had sponsorship from cigarette company John Player & Sons, but our management wouldn't accept sponsorship, so we weren't flash. We were all in different overalls and didn't look very professional but Fred Green, the Triumph sales manager, got some nice overalls for us from Rivett's Leathers so we looked the part.

"Later in the season, when we went to the Bol d'Or, Paul Butler, the Dunlop competition manager, came to see us and asked where our team clothing was. I said that we didn't have any so the next morning he came back with 10 Dunlop jackets, which were much appreciated. They were really nice jackets.

"The triples went well but they grounded out everywhere – and I do mean everywhere. The three-cylinder engine was wider than the twin and so the primary chain case and timing cover grounded all the time.

"Brian Steenson was riding the factory BSA triple, and it was like a sledge, just sliding about from one corner to another. But we had a fix. We rented a garage from a private house up on Mona Drive and there was an old Fiat outside. So, when it was quiet we 'borrowed' one of the bumpers and made protectors for the engine from it. We slipped these between the engine and the fairing. They worked fine and Uphill won the race for us, beating Peter Williams on the factory Norton. ▸

"We all stayed in a little guest house in Douglas, five of us sharing one bedroom. It wasn't very posh but we had a nice breakfast every day – the full Engllish."

"Brian Steenson retired on the BSA and Bob Heath was fifth on the second works BSA, so we knew we had got everything right.

"When we got back to the factory everyone was pleased but there was no champagne or wild party. We'd just done our job, which was to win races for the least possible expenditure–and that's what we'd done."

Despite the success, there was agreement that the frame was dangerously low so it was decided to raise the engine 1⅜in. Today, this would have been a sophisticated piece of computer-aided design, requiring hundreds of hours of meticulous planning: but not at Triumph in 1970.

Les tells the actual story. "When a road bike came back to the service department from a big crash they re-built it totally so the customer effectively got a brand new machine. They were very proud of the level of service they offered to Triumph customers.

"There was one old boy down there who could do anything with a frame. He could straighten anything out, braze it – anything. We went to see him, explained what we wanted and he modified the frame for us and it worked straight away. You could get anything done in the factory if you knew who to ask."

Towards the end of the season, the French Triumph importer pressed the factory to enter the prestigious Bol d'Or, held at L'Autodrome de Linas-Montlhéry, just outside Paris. Tom Dickie and Paul Smart won the event for Triumph, covering 469 laps, a total of 1,838 miles at an average speed of 76.553 mph – a truly incredible performance.

Ironically, the headline was not the Smart/Dickie win but Percy Tait and Steve Jolly who finished fifth, and covered in oil, on the second factory Triumph. So what actually happened in this legendary incident?

Les knows. "The problem started because we were given Duckhams' mineral oil for free, but I wanted to use a castor racing oil because of the extreme valve tip wear we were experiencing. So Duckhams gave us some of their R40 castor oil and we put this into the engines.

"The problem was that castor and mineral oils are not compatible and I think that the castor oil caused a blockage in the oil cooler. This made the engine wet sump and the oil blew out of the engine breather and all over poor old Percy Tait, who was not happy.

"But the bike still finished and we called it 'Slippery Sam' after this."

Slippery Sam won everything there was to win in production racing – so what was the event that Les remembers most fondly?

"When the Triumph factory closed, I was able to buy the bike for £300, which was an awful lot of money for me at the time. I continued to race it under my own name. I spent a lot of time refining the bike until it weighed under 400lbs (181kgs), ready to race.

"For 1975, the Production TT was going to be a 10 lapper and everyone told me not to race the bike. It was a legend,

Triumph Slippery Sam was a big hit with the Brackley crowds.

and to have it blow up and destroy its reputation would have been a tragedy.

"But the bike had done nearly 2,000 miles in one Bol d'Or so I was sure it could manage 10 laps of the 37¾-mile TT course – and it did. Dave Croxford and Alex George won at a race average of 99.61mph and the bike never missed a beat. That was my proudest moment with Slippery Sam."

As a seminal piece of British motorcycle history, Slippery Sam eventually found a permanent home in the National Motorcycle Museum and then, in 2003, disaster struck. A fire swept through the museum and the iconic bike was badly damaged. Les was determined to restore it to its original condition.

"The alloy parts suffered badly but we had some good luck. The original, lightweight fairing was still upstairs in my loft because the bike had been fitted with one of the heavier ones when it was on display in the museum.

"Then, many of the key parts could be salvaged – even down to the oil tank with a dent from where Norman Hyde (a Triumph development engineer who worked with Les) belted it when he fell off in a drag race at Silverstone.

"So no, the bike is not a reproduction, but is the real bike just as we raced it."

Thanks to James Hewing, the National Motorcycle Museum's director, I was given the privilege of riding Slippery Sam in a classic bike demonstration, and while I felt very honoured, I approached the bike with a lot of trepidation.

**1**
**Slippery Sam is a star wherever he appears.**

"Slippery Sam had done nearly 2,000 miles in one Bol d'Or so I was sure it could manage 10 laps of the 37¾ -mile TT course – and it did. We won and that was my proudest moment."

When I got to ride Slippery Sam I was regularly racing a Manx Norton, which was slim and light, and a 500cc Seeley Suzuki, which is positively miniscule: Slippery Sam isn't! In fact, for a race bike, this is a huge motorcycle in terms of width and length. The cockpit is so immense you could have a barbecue in there and not have to come up from behind the fairing.

But it is also a wonderfully practical place to be for long races on fast courses. Its size makes the bike extremely comfortable, and the ergonomics of the controls, fuel tank and handlebars are perfect. If you wanted somewhere perfect to live when you were doing 150mph down Sulby Straight, this would be it.

On the tight little course where I rode the bike, its weight was very apparent, but there was the feeling, given 100mph corners, it would be as stable as the Orient Express.

The engine feels very modern, but in a classic way, with effortless, creamy power and no sense of sharpness. In the dark of the Bol d'Or or the rain and the bumps of the TT course, this is an engine on which you could rely.

In fact, that was the single most important thread running through the whole bike: a racing motorcycle perfectly fit for purpose and worthy of its legendary status. ◆

# Norton Commando 750 – Mk 1

The best of all the Commandos

WHATEVER you think about the Norton Commando, there is one overriding fact that can't be ignored. For a motorcycle which, from its birth, was a stop-gap compromise the Norton Commando was a huge success.

There will never be a precise sales figure, but Mike Jackson, who was Norton's sales manager for most of the Commando's life, estimates something more than 50,000 Commandos were sold – a truly remarkable total for a machine whose engine had been around, in one form or another, for 30 years before the first Commando was sold in 1968.

There is so much Commando history, and myth, that whole books regularly appear about the bike but, in this story, I am going to concentrate on the early 750s which, for my money, are both the best-looking and the most pleasant of all the Commandos.

First, the Commando's bloodline: following the end of the Second World War, every British manufacturer looked at Edward Turner's Triumph Speedtwin with unbridled envy. Turner's 498cc parallel twin ticked every box in the whole motorcycle manufacturing spectrum. It was light, smooth, fast accelerating and drop-dead gorgeous from every angle. That was one side of the coin. ▸

**1**
**There are few sweeter and more useable classic bikes than a 750 Commando.**

**2**
**Early Commandos have an authentically classic appeal while still making a nod to the new world of the 1970s.**

**3**
**Commando frame was, in many ways, a traditional design with a large, stiff spine and duplex engine cradle.**

**4**
**What made the Commando remarkable is Stefan Bauer had the courage to break all accepted motorcycle design principles.**

On the obverse face, there was nothing complicated or difficult to manufacture or design. The Triumph Speedtwin was a simple, push-rod, parallel twin, which was perfectly suited to the limited manufacturing capabilities of the austere post-war years – and every motorcycle company wanted one.

BSA hit the market with their A7. Matchless weighed in with the G9 Super Clubman and Norton commissioned Bert Hopwood to design their take on the parallel twin. To be fair to Hopwood, he was operating in the tightest of straightjackets.

In his book Whatever Happened to the British Motorcycle Industry, Hopwood described his first day at Norton: "Not even during the war time blitzes did I have to work under such difficult circumstances; the whole Norton building was such a slummy shambles, sandwiched with machines and parts, and men and vermin, in a noisy conglomeration.

"My space was not too bad. After all, it was reasonably quiet and did not let in all that much rain."

Hopwood began work as Norton's Chief Designer on April 1, 1947 – All Fools Day – and was immediately tasked with producing a new twin. He had worked with Turner at Triumph and so he knew the Speedtwin's strengths, and weaknesses, very well. In fact, although Hopwood was not a great designer, he did draw a neat, single overhead cam, twin-cylinder engine, which would have made a competitive race bike, as well as a state-of-the-art road machine. It would have been superior to the Speedtwin in every way and just possibly a lifeline for Norton.

However, this motor was killed by a three-pronged attack of internal politics within Norton, a lack of engineering capability and a severe shortage of funds for new tooling. Instead of the new cammy twin, Norton forced Hopwood to produce a conservative 497cc, push-rod twin. It was this engine that was still around in 1967 having been bored and stroked out to 750cc and now rejoicing in the name of the Norton Atlas.

Norton was eventually absorbed by Associated Motor Cycles, which owned a whole garage full of iconic brands, led by Norton, Matchless and AJS. Along with the rest of the British motorcycle industry, utterly inept management brought the whole empire to its knees.

In 1967, British entrepreneur Dennis Poore bought the ashes of this once great company for what wasn't much more than two balloons and a goldfish, and incorporated it within his umbrella company, Manganese Bronze Holdings.

The star jewel in AMC's very dented crown was the Norton brand. Racing had ruined the company with more than 90% of the factory's very limited R&D budget being spent on competition machines just after the Second World War – at a time when the Birmingham factory desperately needed a new range of road bikes. However, world championship success had kept the Norton name alive in the buying public's eyes so this was the brand Poore decided would be his flagship.

The problem was that the only flag Norton had in its locker that was half-worth putting on to any ship, was the painfully old-fashioned Norton Atlas – still powered by the grandchild of Hopwood's 1947 push-rod twin.

Norton aficionados will tell you the Atlas is a rooty-tooty-shoot-from-the-hip-git-them-longhorns-amovin real man's motorcycle. Sadly, it's not.

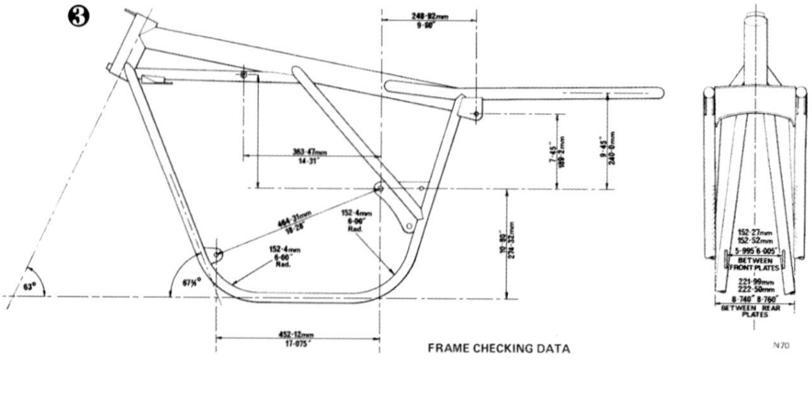

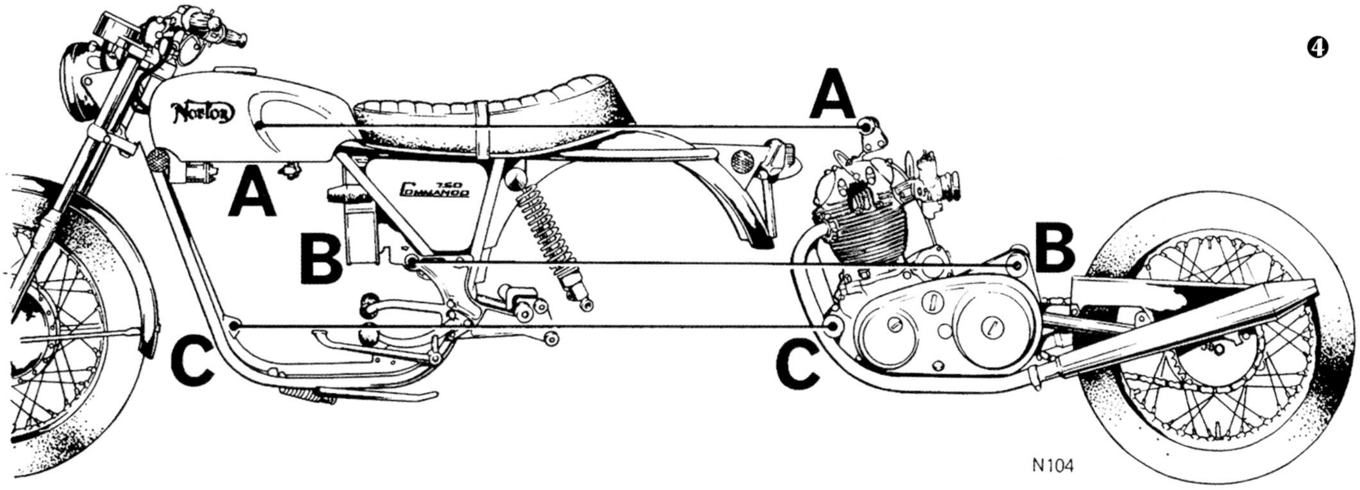


In fact, the Atlas is a rough old thing and not a patch on either the BSA Golden Flash or Triumph's super sexy Bonneville. You can't blame Hopwood because, at 745cc, the Atlas was vastly too big to be smooth and, mounted in the Norton Featherbed frame, the centre of gravity was also too high for good handling. In fact, with 1960s tyres, the Atlas would really snap out of line when ridden hard.

I know this from personal experience. My friend Alan let me have a ride on his Atlas and, of course, I had to give him a full demonstration of why I was a teenage MotoGod. I was really having a 'big go' through the 'twisties' on the Mold to Denbigh road when I just caught an ever so slightly damp patch with the Atlas' rear wheel – and, goodness me, did that thing give me a thrill! Alan had seen the whole incident and, at Denbigh, took his bike back from me in sullen silence, which I thought was a bit hard because I had caught a bottom-clencher of a slide – and stayed on! Some people just don't know when to be grateful.

Difficult though it might be to believe, back at Manganese Bronze, Dennis Poore had bigger issues than even assessing my riding ability or Alan's sulks. He looked at what was on offer in terms of engineering ability at AMC – and promptly hired his own staff.

There was not exactly an over-abundance of talent in the British bike industry so Poore head-hunted his chief engineer, Dr Stefan Bauer, from Rolls Royce, which was knee-deep in world-leading designers.

He turned to Austin cars for development engineer Bob Trigg, and moved Bernard Hooper and John Favill from Villiers engines, another company which Poore owned, to the Norton project.

Bauer took one look at the Atlas engine, housed in the Featherbed frame, and threw up his hands in despair. Not only did the bike look very dated – this was the end of the 'Swinging '60s' and everything had to be cutting edge–but a 30-year-old engine, in a 28-year-old chassis didn't look much like a guaranteed sales success either. ▸

"Not even during the war time blitzes did I have to work in such a slummy shambles as Norton."

Not that the bad news stopped with the Atlas. AMC had spent a lot of time and money on the Norton P10 project and, in many ways, this was far worse than Hopwood's parallel twin. On paper, the 800cc P10 was a thoroughly modern engine with a unit construction, five-speed gearbox and double overhead cams. In practice, it was a disaster. The ludicrously long cam chain was almost impossible to fit on a production line and stretched in use; the engine leaked oil and it didn't make any more power than the Atlas. In short, its primary value was as scrap metal.

The big plan was to make an all new twin – water-cooled, electric start and unit construction – but, even if everything went perfectly, this was a two-year project and Poore needed something to sell immediately.

Bauer came up with an engineer's solution by playing the weak hand of cards he had been given, very carefully. It was impossible to eliminate the harsh vibration of the Atlas engine – and it really is coarse – but how about if you could hide it from the rider? Now that just might work…

The first step was to consign the Featherbed frame to the history books, where it belonged, and Dr Bauer came up with a real peach of a design to replace it.

The heart of the bike was a huge, 2¼in (57mm) top spine which provided ample torsional rigidity. A Featherbed-ish duplex loop dropped down from the spine. This design enabled the engine to be much further forward than in the Featherbed and, in most cases, the nearer the engine is to the front wheel, the better the bike steers. The Atlas engine could also now be canted further forward, which was a huge styling aid.

Clever as the new spine frame was, the magic lay in how Bauer mounted the engine. In an act of sheer garden shed engineering genius, the good doctor did no more than tie the engine, the separate gearbox and the swinging arm together, in one contiguous unit isolated from the rest of the frame on a series of bonded rubber bushes named Isolastics.

If mounting the engine on rubber bushes was bold then tying the swinging arm into the gearbox and engine, but not the frame, was ground-breaking to the point of being reckless, or so many motorcycling experts of the time felt. To be fair, it was highly counter-intuitive. Swinging arms were, and are, supposed to be precisely in line with the frame, and how could this be done if they were mounted on bits of wobbly rubber?

Except that they weren't.

The bushes were almost solid and were kept precisely in place by polyurethane thrust washers, which severely restricted side play. A perfectly set up Commando really does handle well and, equally, once the engine is above 2,500(ish) rpm, most vibrations don't reach the rider.

As with so many British bikes, the devil is in the detail, and what a naughty little imp the Commando can be. The load that the thrust washers apply to the bushes is controlled by

shims – extremely thin pieces of metal. Overload the thrust washers and it's welcome to vibe central – under tension them and the Commando will wander all over the road like a first-year student coming out of their first Freshers' party. Yet, like Goldilocks, a skilled Commando tuner will neither over nor under shim the bushes, but will just perfectly hit the sweet tension spot–at which point, the Commando really does work.

Not that Bauer solved all the problems on paper. Following his engineering drawings precisely, the first frames frequently broke and it took the development skills of Bob Trigg and Bernard Hooper to make the design work as a mass-produced item.

The Commando was launched at the 1967 Earls Court Bike Show with a lovely silver paint job and a funny, rather new age, green blob on the tank. One can only presume the designer was partaking of some herbal medicine when he sketched that one!

The seat was a very hippy, orangey-red and the rear of the bike had a lovely faired in tail unit. In my fluorescent pink shirt, flower tie and flared trousers I thought it was great. The pipe-smoking, Barbour-jacket wearing, establishment motorcycle chaps recoiled in horror – condemning the new bike as not a real Norton but the spawn of the devil.

Had the aficionados stood back for just a moment, they would have realised just how wrong they were. For a start, there was the Atlas engine in all its oil-leaking, vibrating, vulgar glory. The gearbox was a separate four-speeder and, heaven protect us, there was clearly no sign of an electric starter.

The front forks were standard Norton Roadholder, as was the front hub, but with a hastily added twin leading shoe brake plate. In fact, the Commando was very much a traditional British bike in every way.

Ironically, this is why I am rather fond of the very early Commandos. Later manifestations of the bike start to become, dare I say it, slightly modern with left-hand gear change and electric starters. Or, more accurately, electric but-only-on-a-very-good-day starters.

In the middle, the 828cc Combat-engined bikes are harsh, shouty things, which swear in front of ladies and spit on pavements. Not my sort of motorcycle at all.

**1**
**The Commando engine has strong family ties to Bert Hopwood's first Norton twin of 1947.**

By contrast, the Isolastic system does work ever so well with the 750cc engine and can be refined even further with the addition of the later vernier adjustment system. Electronic ignition, now retro-fitted to almost every Commando in existence, means kick starting is no longer the chore it once was and, with the passage of time, everyone agrees these first Commandos really are rather good looking.

Finally, owning a Commando is a sheer delight. The bikes are easy to work on and the spares supply is the best for any classic motorcycle in existence. In fact, it is so good you can still order a brand-new Commando either in standard form or modernised, as the mood takes you.

Commandos are also good value: £8,000 will buy you a really nice 750, which will invariably have been well sorted out by now. The bike will steer and handle beautifully and will cruise all day at 70mph – even two up.

In short, it is a lot of bike for the money and one which will be utterly depreciation proof, too.

Thanks to Lawrence Rose of Classic Motorcycles Ltd (classicbikes1@yahoo.co.uk) ◆

RACER

# Moto Guzzi V7-II

If only I'd had this bike when I was 16 years old

The backstory to this report on the V7 is that we – Carol, who is my wife and photographer, and I – were doing a job for MV Agusta at their Schiranna works, right on the banks of Lake Varese. As an aside, MV have the world's most beautiful location for a motorcycle factory, literally next to the lake, which was the test site for the Macchi seaplanes: absolutely idyllic.

This area of Italy is, or was, the centre of the Italian bike industry, with the iconic MV Agusta race bikes being made just down the road from Schiranna in the Agusta Bell helicopter site, at Cascina Costa.

Gilera were at Arcore, fittingly almost next to the Monza race circuit, and the legendary FB Mondial company was a bit further east at Manerbio.

But, back to the V7...

For me, the greatest of the legendary Italian manufacturers was Moto Guzzi, whose headquarters at Mandello del Lario are so close to Lake Como that you can almost touch the water from the main doors. Importantly for us, Mandello del Lario is only 50 miles away from Schiranna and so was very easily accessible once we had finished the job we were doing with MV.

Why do I think so highly of Moto Guzzi? Quite simply, the factory was not only the great success story of Italian motorcycle manufacturing in terms of sales and profitability They were outstandingly the leader in motorcycle technology, with a world championship success record which proved this.

At its peak in the 1950s and 1960s, Guzzi was the only motorcycle company in the world to have a wind tunnel. They were working on bike aerodynamics at a time when the science was confined exclusively to aircraft and a very few exotic cars.

Guzzi also produced the most amazing motorcycle of all time – the incredible 500cc, eight-cylinder 'Otto', which was conceived in 1954 by Guzzi's resident design genius, Giulio Cesare Carcano. There has never been a more impressive motorcycle engine designed before or since.

Freelance journalists are always keeping an eye on potential sales of stories so the idea was that I would visit the Moto Guzzi museum and write an article about this wonderful, quirky homage to Guzzi's history.

Guzzi is now owned by the giant Piaggio Group, and so my enquiry had to go through their press department. The chap handling the enquiry was very courteous, but was adamant the museum was closed to visitors. No ifs, buts or maybes: just closed for the foreseeable future.

But I did have one secret, ace card to play: I am one of the very, very few people in the world to have ridden a Moto Guzzi V8. This immense privilege came about through the good grace of Sammy Miller, who has an 'Otto' in his museum's collection – and he actually *did* let me ride the bike.

I mentioned this to the Piaggio press officer and he was, at first, justifiably sceptical. Then I sent him the pictures of me on the bike. Suddenly the sun came out and the museum was opened up for a private visit and guided tour, conducted by one of the old Guzzi staff. It was an immense privilege and one for which I will remain forever grateful.

But this was only the first part of Piaggio's generosity. As well as opening up the museum they offered me the chance to ride their best-selling retro bike – the V7-II. And all this on a brilliant, Italian summer's day. What could possibly go wrong?

In the morning, we had the museum tour followed by an excellent lunch. The atmosphere was super relaxed and the agreement was I could ride the V7 for as long as I wished and then we would all have a bite to eat to finish off the day.

Everything was going really well as we rode up into the mountains opposite Mandello del Lario. Fortunately, a lifetime of paranoia made me insist on doing some action shots quite early in the test. 'Things', in all of fate's wonderful panoply of cock-ups, often happen when testing a bike and no more so when the job seems to be 101% perfect.

So we got one set of pics boxed off, with the intention of riding for a couple of hours more and getting a second lot from the top of the mountain.

Then our minder got a phone call from his girlfriend – really – and the dynamic changed in half a nano second. Now, we had to get the bike back to the Guzzi factory in triple quick time.

Off went the Guzzi PR bloke with a style and speed that would have put him on the podium at the TT. This was fine but I wasn't exactly sure where the Guzzi factory was – and all our clothes, money, passports and car keys were inside waiting for us.

I could see the very real possibility of camping out next to the V7 in the car park by the Piazza Carlo Guzzi and perhaps begging a meal by offering to do the washing up.

The only solution was to hang on to the number plate of our guide's bike and forget speed limits, traffic and everything else. ▸

V twin engine
is unmistakably
Moto Guzzi.

I was a very handy road racer at one time, but although I never got a trophy for the race back to Mandello del Lario, I put this as one of my best ever rides – two-up and with Carol carrying a bag full of camera gear!

You don't have to be mad to be a freelancer etc...

However, before the race back to the factory I was becoming ever fonder of the V7. To be honest, I'm not a big fan of the wider retro scene. It must be an age thing, but I think anyone who pays a premium for a pair of torn jeans really has more money than sense.

The same applies to fake classic bikes. Some classic machines were excellent. Even today, I have never ridden a more involving and satisfying bike than a Matchless G.50, and if I never rode another machine other than a 1962 Triumph Trophy I would be happy. However, most classic bikes were rubbish – unreliable, difficult to start and with predictably unpredictable handling and power which wouldn't excite a torpid hamster. To copy these bikes is just as silly as wearing a brand new t-shirt which has been mechanically aged.

This is why I am reluctant to put the Moto Guzzi V7-II into the retro bike segment because, rather than being a parody of a classic motorcycle it is a very, very fine modern motorcycle in its own right and yet one which still carries almost 100 years of motorcycle manufacturing heritage.

Let's begin by looking at what makes a classic bike better than a modern machine – when on paper it should lose out on every front. The key, overwhelmingly important factor is the motorcycle must have an emotional link to the rider. This is where many retro bikes miss out. Adding complexity to a motorcycle does not automatically make it better – it just makes it more complex.

There is no argument that if you have a 200hp superbike cranked right over, and on the very limits of tyre adhesion, you either need a vast amount of talent or a lot of rider aids. There is a less valid, but still credible, argument for having different mapping options on your heavily laden AT machine as you ride from warm, dry roads into monsoon conditions.

However, what the electronics do for most riders is to separate them from the very reason they ride in the first place – the pursuit of that unique link which comes only when there is a truly anthropomorphic bond between rider and motorcycle – the two-wheeled horse in living metal. The best, and only the very best, young designers understand this very subtle and nuanced idea, and when they produce a modern classic it retains all the intense involvement of an old classic – but adds an electric starter and a lack of oil puddles on the garage floor.

> "I was a very handy road racer at one time. Although I never got a trophy for the race back to Mandello del Lario, I put this as one of my best rides – two up and with Carol carrying a bag full of camera gear! You don't have to be mad to be a freelancer etc..."

The heart of the V7 is the transverse v-twin engine – and this power unit really has earned its oats for Moto Guzzi over the last 50 odd years. To an untrained eye, the transverse engine v-twin looks just like every other Guzzi that has used this car engine since 1967. However, in the last half century, things have moved on vastly. Yes, the engine does lie, uniquely among modern, mass-produced motorcycles, in a 90° V across the frame and yes, it is air-cooled, but the latest manifestation of the concept is very modern and comes with all the obligatory emissions control in the form of a catalytic converter and fuel injection.

However, despite being compliant with all current and predicted legislation, Guzzi has done a very clever job in that the cat converter is completely inconspicuous and the twin exhausts have a suitably classic growl to them. In fact, it's better than this. If you are so inclined, you could creep round a Trappist monastery quadrangle and not disturb the monks' contemplation.

Alternatively, you can have a lot of fun!

Give the V7 a seriously sporting handful of throttle and the over-square, 80mm x 94mm, 744cc v-twin has a really pleasant growl. It's not the angry Rottweiler of a lightly silenced Norton Commando, but certainly enough aural pleasure to give the impression bureaucrats haven't stifled all the pleasure out of riding a retro bike.

The engine itself is a lovely thing and is as effective as it is visually attractive. This is very much a motor to be seen, stroked and admired, and so it is important the castings and machining are both impeccable – which they are. The power the V7 produces is very deceptive. Clearly, the V7 has to be compliant with European A2 licence requirements so it

**V7 attracted fans wherever it was stopped.**

produces 48hp @ rpm. Now this doesn't sound like much fun, but it is, because Guzzi have somehow managed to get peak torque at an incredibly low 3,000rpm. In practice, having this much pulling power available means the V7 can be ridden like a scooter or, heaven forbid, a cruiser.

The latest versions of the V7 come with an optional, additional 7hp through some tweaking of the engine mapping.

Our test route took us up some serious hills surrounding Lake Como and, carrying me and Carol, who was taking the images for the story, the V7 was a perfectly practical touring machine.

Where it lost out was on top speed. I have no idea what the V7's actual, head-buried-in-the-tank maximum is – but I would be surprised if it is much north of 105mph. Returning to the Guzzi factory, I saw 95mph on the speedometer half a dozen times. At these speeds, the V7's aerodynamics – those of a porcine brick – start to demand power that the bike clearly doesn't have.

But here is the core of the matter. With an increasing number of 50mph speed limits, 90mph is going to get you the much-loved ban, so at what point does the top speed become merely a matter of geeky conjecture? For absolutely certain, I could ride the V7 hard all day two-up and stretch the tolerance of the law to the outer limits with the 48hp.

However, a bit more urge would be nice, and after the test was completed we were gossiping to Guzzi staff. Someone mentioned the factory does have a rather special V7 currently wandering around northern Italy. This engine knocks out 65hp, has even more torque, and really would tick all the boxes.

I think Guzzi are still unsure about a hot V7, which is slightly odd because Triumph have no problem with the properly sporty Thruxton R. Probably the biggest problem the bike faces is the constant machinations within the Piaggio Group, which is at a level that would make Niccolò Machiavelli proud.

Back to the present and the V7 gearbox and clutch. At one time, in the good – actually bad – old days, selecting a gear on a Guzzi was a real lucky dip affair. Yes, it was possible to get a Guzzi 'box working properly, but only with the efforts of a skilled tuner and a sensitive rider. By contrast, the six-speed V7 is a thoroughly modern gearbox, with sweet, effortless selection. I never once missed a gear, up or down, and that would have been an impossible thing to write even a few years ago. The six-speeder might be considered overkill on a bike like the V7, but in the real world, it isn't. The ratio spacing is now ideal in all conditions from trickling through traffic to fast riding.

The single plate clutch is light and grab free, and the shaft drive unobtrusive.

**1**
**Minimalist instrument panel and traditional racing fly screen were lovely.**

**2**
**The V7 11 is a real quirky, original delight in a world of conformity.**

In 2015, the engine was tilted forward by 4° and lowered by 10mm (a bit under ½in). This gives the bike a more pleasing look and also provides 3cm (more than an inch) of extra clearance behind the heads and barrels, which is always welcome for the long of leg. At 5ft 11in, I never found the motor intrusive.

The saddle has also been lowered to 790mm (31in). Normally, this rings warning bells for me since, with racing-knackered knees, I can't manage a cramped riding position. There was no problem at all, with plenty of room being available. Carol also commented on having ample space for the pillion. ▸

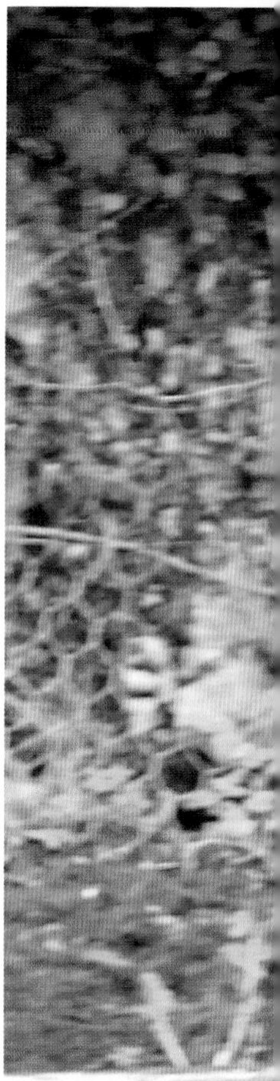

The chassis is another case of Guzzi understanding what it is doing in terms of the V7. Compared to an Aprilia Superbike – Aprilia being Piaggio's other key motorcycle brand – the Guzzi is basic to the point of being crude. It has a steel frame and no adjustment on the suspension worth talking about. Only the alloy swinging arm is vaguely modern. The rear end has twin Bitubo shocks and, again, these are fine.

Including the twin shocks, there is nothing – as in absolutely nothing – wrong with this chassis. All the top classic race bikes use steel frames and swinging arms, and they will out handle most modern Superbikes. The wear on my boots' toe sliders indicated the V7 will provide plenty of fun.

Guzzi doesn't publish steering geometry figures, but the lovely, neutral handling feel of the bike suggests it won't be far off the magical 63° and 2½in (63mm) of trail that defines perfect classic motorcycle handling.

The braking is fine, too. It's not up to Superbike standards, but coming down off the hills, two up, there was plenty of power just in the 320mm front disc alone.

Some journalists have been all snotty and hormonal about the ABS and traction control, which the V7 now has. Who needs TC with so little power? I have a different view. Many V7s will be used by riders with very little riding experience, so why not protect them as they come to terms with their first full-sized bike? Sliding down the road because you have lost traction on either wheel doesn't enhance the riding experience in any way.

Finally, but still of critical importance in this market sector, the whole V7 range is beautifully finished. Someone has taken care with the design details on these bikes, and Piaggio accountants haven't screwed the last penny out of production costs – and it shows. There are reasons for this policy. The V7 range are uniquely Guzzi's bikes, not derivatives from another part of the Piaggio empire, and customers world-wide like them. Rather than being a niche product, like Honda's CB1100EX, the V7s are paying Guzzi's bills.

There is a big idea behind the range, and this is where I disagree with Guzzi. The V7s come in three flavours, ranging from the Stone 'Bagger' to my favourite, which was Racer. All the bikes are mechanically identical. This needs stressing. Regardless of what your V7 looks like, it will go, handle and stop just the same as every other V7. Personally, I don't like the matt paint finish on the Stone. If you can't polish your retro bike its whole *raison d'etre* is questionable – and Guzzi could provide you with a paint job so deep and lustrous you would want to swim in it.

So, my choice of tank would be the chrome job from the Racer. This would be great because I like the dropped 'bars on the Racer, too. The problem is the Racer only has a single seat and so Carol can't ride with me. Guzzi's answer is I should buy a dual seat and have the dealer fit it for me before delivery – and then sell the single seat to recoup the cost.

Likewise, instead of the basic simplicity of putting a different-coloured fuel tank on a V7 – I would have to buy the 'standard' tank and retro-fit the one I actually want.

This policy is in stark contrast with how Triumph sells their retros, where accessories/customisation are added at the point of sale by the dealer

All the options – exhausts, seats, tanks – fit on any V7 without any modification, and not even ECU re-mapping is required. This being the case, why can't a customer simply order the bike he or she wants directly from the production line? It's hardly a new idea. The vast majority of new cars are now built to order and to hugely more complex demands. Car customers can specify the engine, internal trim and every other bell and whistle in the catalogue, or not, as their budget

**1**
**A real delight for children of all ages.**

**2**
**You'll need a plentiful supply of toe sliders if you ride the V7 hard – which you should!**

permits – but all the options will go on to one chassis.

I can see the accountants' eye view of selling lots of after-market accessories to V7 owners, but I think that Guzzi would do better by letting buyers customise the bikes directly from the production line and then, if they want to add clutch and brake levers machined from unobtainium billet, let them indulge their fantasies privately.

This brings us to the big question – how does the V7 fare against the rest of the retro market opposition? The answer is outstandingly well – in its niche. I am really very fond of Triumph's Street Twin, but the V7 does provide a credible alternative to the smallest Bonneville.

It's not fair to compare the 744cc V7 with the much larger capacity 1200cc Triumph Speed Twin or the very highly specified, and expensive Thruxton R, which is almost a separate category in its own right.

The Royal Enfield Bullets are okay, but 29hp really is a cure for insomnia. I once had a lawnmower with a tuned two-stroke engine – and that made more power than a Bullet!

The Royal Enfield Interceptor is a much, much better bet, and is very much a competitor for the V7. I prefer the Guzzi – but, there again, I want a Guzzi V8 as my race bike.

The Ducati Scrambler range I like too, and the bikes are very stylish and go extremely well. The problem is they are a size too small for me and I couldn't imagine riding one all day.

So, the V7 isn't the best retro bike on sale today, but it's right on the pace for its price and performance sector. For sure, I would have one for our road bike.

No, that's a fib. I wouldn't – because I like our 1000cc Ducati Classic Sport too much, but that's only because I normally ride two-up with Carol – and I'm too old now to grow up and be sensible! ◆

# Honda Rune

## Not for the shy

THE whole idea of what constitutes a classic is getting ever more blurred – and this is right and proper.

What is iconic to an ancient like me is often, at best, nothing more than quirky and confusing to someone born in the 1990s. I have no issue with this at all – none whatsoever – because every generation must find magic in what they do and achieve, rather than trying to relive the glories of the past.

Equally, I hope the bikes in this book transcend particular eras because they are all true classics in their own way – and none more so than the Honda NRX 1800, known to its acolytes all over the world as the Rune.

I have to confess a touch of a racism at this point – but only of the motorcycling kind. I really don't like the custom scene and silly bikes with half a gnat's eyelash of ground clearance, a chocolate exhaust pipe and no mudguards.

They might be art, whatever that means, but these things are joyless creatures and can never capture the exhilaration of motorcycling. How can you have any fun on bike that won't go round corners, won't stop and needs cleaning every 10 minutes?

This explains why you wouldn't normally find me on a bike like the Honda Rune – which truly is custom bike high art. The reason I did ride the bike was because of Sean Davies, the sales manager at the very fine Knutsford Honda dealership, which is now, sadly, gone from the bike scene.

Sean was a hard core real motorcycle fan, just like me, and had taken the Rune in part exchange against a sports bike. It was sitting in the dealership, totally dominating the whole showroom floor, and I began to make my normal, smarty pants comments about what rubbish all custom bikes are.

Sean put his arm round me, smiled and said: "Not this one. This is a bike you need to ride and then come back and tell me what you think..."

This is why I, a hard-core sports bike and classic racer fan, found myself sitting just 27 inches (680 mm) from the floor on a motorcycle that is nearly 7ft (1830 mm) long and weighs in at an eye-watering 850lbs plus. I am never over-awed by riding test bikes, but the Rune is simply so much motorcycle I had a real sense of trepidation when I eased in first gear and prepared to carefully let out the clutch to launch this truly amazing motorcycle.

The Rune is – first, last and middle – an American dream. After visiting the Tokyo Show in 1995, and seeing the Honda Japan-designed Zodiac concept bike, Honda Research America began thinking about where the custom cruiser concept could be taken.

The Zodiac was a v-twin and the immediate problem was any v-twin, no matter how good, always runs into the accusation that it is trying to be a Harley-Davidson. However, the Zodiac was radically styled, with the trailing link forks being particularly striking.

Back in California, the HRA designers did have one ace card to play: the truly awesome, flat- six Honda motor, which powered both the Gold Wing and Valkyrie. No-one, and particularly not Harley, had anything like this power plant at their disposal. ▸

**1**
**Honda Rune trailing link forks make a real engineering statement.**

**2**
**T4 concept bike.**

"The Rune is so vast that you probably need a truck driving licence to ride it."

2

1

HONDA

Cornering a Rune is more like yacht sailing than motorcycling – smooth and steady gets you through the turn!

The six-cylinder engine powered Honda's flagship Gold Wing super-tourer – a motorcycle so vast you can take not only your partner for a week's holiday but also a couple of kids and the family dog. The Wing also has a very clear identity, which is based on being huge, immensely well specified, and providing every conceivable luxury – including a raft of totally unnecessary ones.

The Gold Wing also had a little sister – younger and much slimmer. This was the F6C Valkyrie, basically a Wing which had been on a diet and wore, compared to its sibling, minimalist clothing.

Honda America loaned a Valkyrie to me when I was visiting them, and Carol and I rode it almost down to the Mexican border and back. I quite liked the bike because its six-cylinder engine is unique, and highly addictive, but it did feel what it was – a stripped down Gold Wing that wasn't a Gold Wing. I enjoyed riding the bike, but not enough to make me lust after one.

The problem was that the Valkyrie feels like a motorcycle which someone with a lot of money – an awful lot – could get a talented specials' builder to make, and this was not what Honda wanted. Not at all.

I wasn't the only one who felt that way. Executive VP of Honda America, Ray Blank, was a strong supporter of the as-yet unnamed super cruiser and said: "We wanted to extend this concept (a motorcycle based on the Valkyrie/Gold Wing power plant) once again and take another cutting-edge motorcycle into uncharted territory, establishing new directions that no other manufacturer had ever attempted.

"We wanted to set the bar higher than ever, erecting standards that no one else had yet imagined, while also exploding old limitations on what an original equipment manufacturer could mass produce."

These were all big ideas but honest ones, coming as they did from someone with a powerful position within the world's biggest, and arguably most innovative, motorcycle manufacturer.

Honda America produced four Valkyrie-based prototypes to test public reaction. These ranged from a mild, close relative of the Valkyrie, labelled T1, all the way to the hugely aggressive Hot-Rod T4. In the middle was T2 – a motorcycle quite unlike anything seen before or since.

At this point, it becomes all too easy to fall down the abyss that is marketing and design hype. The Honda press release at the time described the Rune as having a "Neo-retro persona" – and you just know anything carrying this label isn't going to be on sale in the bargain aisle of your local Poundshop.

Incredibly, 'neo-retro' isn't a bad description. What Honda means is the Rune is the sort of thing you might see in a sci-fi movie, set in some imaginary 1930s parallel universe – maybe Batman with a touch less aggression.

Above all else, the Rune was designed to be looked at – and then the appearance was transformed into a useable motorcycle.

**Batman's personal retro bike.**

Ray Blank again: "You have to remember that Honda's greatest strength is its engineering ability. Function, horsepower, performance, durability – a lot of very measurable qualities.

"But now here we were, championing the production of what was essentially a one-off custom special, a show bike with a whole set of gut-level aesthetic qualities, which are impossible to measure.

"The Rune concept is extremely extravagant, because it places the highest priorities on style rather than measurable science and engineering, and that created challenges during product planning.

"It is a very emotional product. But when a gut feeling is so strong, avid motorcyclists can communicate with one another on a different level. We accomplished a lot on this new concept after hours, at restaurants, just motorcycle guys talking to each other, scribbling on napkins, waving our hands around."

So the Americans had their way: an utterly radical custom motorcycle, which you could order straight off the showroom floor from your friendly local Honda dealer. The problem now was to make what would have been a truly impressive feat for a one-off custom bike builder into a machine that would go into series production. This was not an easy task.

Back in Japan, Masanori Aoki was chosen as Project Leader. Aoki had come from a sports bike background and wasn't discomforted by the technical challenges. Rather, what caused the unease was starting the design process from what appeared to be the wrong end – especially at Honda, where engineering is king. Instead of beginning with a series of performance targets, working towards them with engineering solutions and then finally allowing the stylists to finish off the job, the appearance of the Rune dominated the process.

Did it matter if the Rune had a top speed of 115mph, 120mph or 125mph? Not in the slightest.

Was trimming the weight by 25lbs going to affect the bike? Not at all.

Appearance, sound and image were the holy trinity.

Not that the engineering was simple. Although the Gold Wing engine was now a whopping 1832cc, it was still a very mild, inoffensive unit.

Aoki gave the monster lump a good tweaking with new cams, a re-mapped ignition and six individual fuel injectors, all of which resulted in 118hp and a truly eye-popping 123ft lbs of torque – equating to roughly 50% more torque than a Honda Fireblade of the day. Now, the Rune had a Gold Wing power plant with attitude.

Mr Aoki was also keen to bring in sports bike technology in terms of the chassis. The rear suspension is Honda Pro-link, which is both extremely neat and provides an element of rising rate in the 3.8in (96mm) of travel.

Following customer demands, Aoki retained the trailing link front suspension. Previously, this had only been used successfully on sidecar motocross outfits, but the beauty of it with the Rune is it gives the front end the impression of being very heavily raked – almost chopper style – while in actual fact retaining almost conventional steering geometry.

The fork is a mass of castings, bushes and dampers, and must have cost a fortune to make. In practical terms it is probably less effective than a conventional telescopic front end but there is no argument about the visual statement it makes: Honda does clever engineering, and makes it work, so never forget that Milwaukee!

Where Aoki wouldn't be distracted by styling was in the safety element of the Rune; the weight and size of it needs putting into perspective. At around 850lbs ready to roll, the Rune is more than one third of the weight of a small Honda car, and the motorcycle will slaughter the automobile in terms of performance. For example, the Rune will run up to more than 120mph and will manage 0-100 in a shade more than 11 seconds. This is no 'Easy Rider', Stetson-wearing cruiser, but something quite different.

In order to stop this behemoth, Aoki fitted twin 330mm front discs with three pad callipers. The hydraulics are also set up so a firm two fingers are all that is required to put the Titanic's propellers in reverse and bring what is a very large, and surprisingly fast, motorcycle under control. Once again, it is clever but so subtle engineering.

However, what dominates the bike is its stunning finish. There are very few custom bike builders anywhere in the world that could even match, let alone surpass, the quality of the chrome and paintwork on the Rune.

So this brings us to the pre-launch chat I received from Sean. He was all smiles and encouragement, but there is no forgetting this was a very expensive motorcycle I was sitting on – and needed treating with care.

This is an interesting conundrum about Runes. First, they are invariably in unbelievably mint condition. No-one bought a Rune to go trail riding or even for nipping out for fish and chips. ▸

Second, for the same reason they are always low mileage. Together, these factors mean that a 15-year-old Rune has hardly depreciated from its new price. Today, you are not going to own any Rune for less than £10,000, and a top drawer one will cost another £5,000 on top of this.

The only downside is repair costs are horrendous. Each Rune left the American Honda Plant at Marysville, Ohio, costing the company a reported $100,000 – and sold for just a quarter of that price. Honda has to get the money back somehow and therefore repairing a Rune is never going to be a cheap exercise.

Watched by a gaggle of Knutsford Honda staff, I make triple-certain the road is completely empty, feed in the clutch – and then watch as the front of the bike leaves the parking lot followed by me, and the rest of the motorcycle, in what seems like a considerably long time. This is a seriously huge motorcycle!

Once moving, and with thoughts of crashing the bike and having to sell both of my kidneys to pay for the repairs put to the back of my mind, it becomes apparent the Rune is a very clever motorcycle indeed.

For a start, the flat six engine is a joy – a real gem. Possessing unbelievable torque, combined with silky smoothness, the motor provides a magic carpet experience. A glance at the neo-retro (and I do like that adjective), digital speedometer reveals the feeling is reflected in the facts: 70mph is available in a blink and 90mph is there at will. Dull this bike most certainly isn't.

The exhaust note is intoxicating. The nearest equivalent is a small jet turbine. Stand at an airport perimeter fence as a Lear Jet rolls by and you will be in the same aural ball park as the Rune.

The gearbox and clutch are typically Honda sweet, the brakes are everything one could ask for, and the shaft drive is completely innocuous. Even the apparently silly riding position is practical – although I can never see the attraction of having one's arms spread out crucifixion style: perhaps I am not sufficiently religiously inclined.

The problem comes with the handling. Even easing the bike into corners, it has a most disconcerting habit of skipping over irregularities in the road surface. The first time the Rune does this seriously is at the joint between the concrete and tarmac on the M56 access road. The front end of the Rune skips – and my heart stops. A quarter of a ton of bike ploughing into the Armco – and I'm going to die with it!

Slowly, over a period of maybe 30 miles, I realise the fault is not so much with the bike as with me. Despite having 50 years of riding experience on every motorcycle known to mankind I am making the classic beginner's mistake of being too tense. I simply need to relax and let the bike do its own thing.

So the next time the Rune skips and shakes its head, I do absolutely nothing – and the bike ploughs on effortlessly. It has to be said that all corners are still something to be taken very seriously on a Rune – but they are neither traumatic or dangerous. The Rune is no supersports bike – but it is a million times better than a custom cruiser.

Trick suspension or not, the ride on the Rune is mediocre. Again, it's no doubt better than mainstream custom bikes, but ride a Rune more than 50 miles and you will get aches in the bum, spine, and shoulders. The fuel tank is also far too wide and has a ludicrously large capacity at six gallons. Six gallons equates to a cruising range of nearly 200 miles, and no-one is going to ride a Rune this far unless they are being pursued by aliens looking for their motorcycle to be returned. Is the pleasure worth the pain? Read on...

In all the years I have been reporting on motorcycles, I have never, ever seen the reaction to a bike like the one we had at the Rune photo shoot. If we had parked Tom Cruise on the Rune the crowds wouldn't have been denser. Quite simply, if you want to be the focus of attention then buy a Rune: it is the epicentre of the whole multiverse in terms of motorcycling narcissism.

Ironically, it is also a cheap motorcycle to own – providing you are a major shareholder in a polish manufacturing company and don't crash it. The word in the bike trade is Runes are *not* depreciating–they are actually *going up* in value – and that's a rare feat outside the thoroughbred classic bike world.

And here's a final thought… If the book you are reading becomes an international best seller, with a million copies going through the till, then I actually do think I would own a Rune. How's that for a recommendation from a hard-core classic sports bike man? ◆

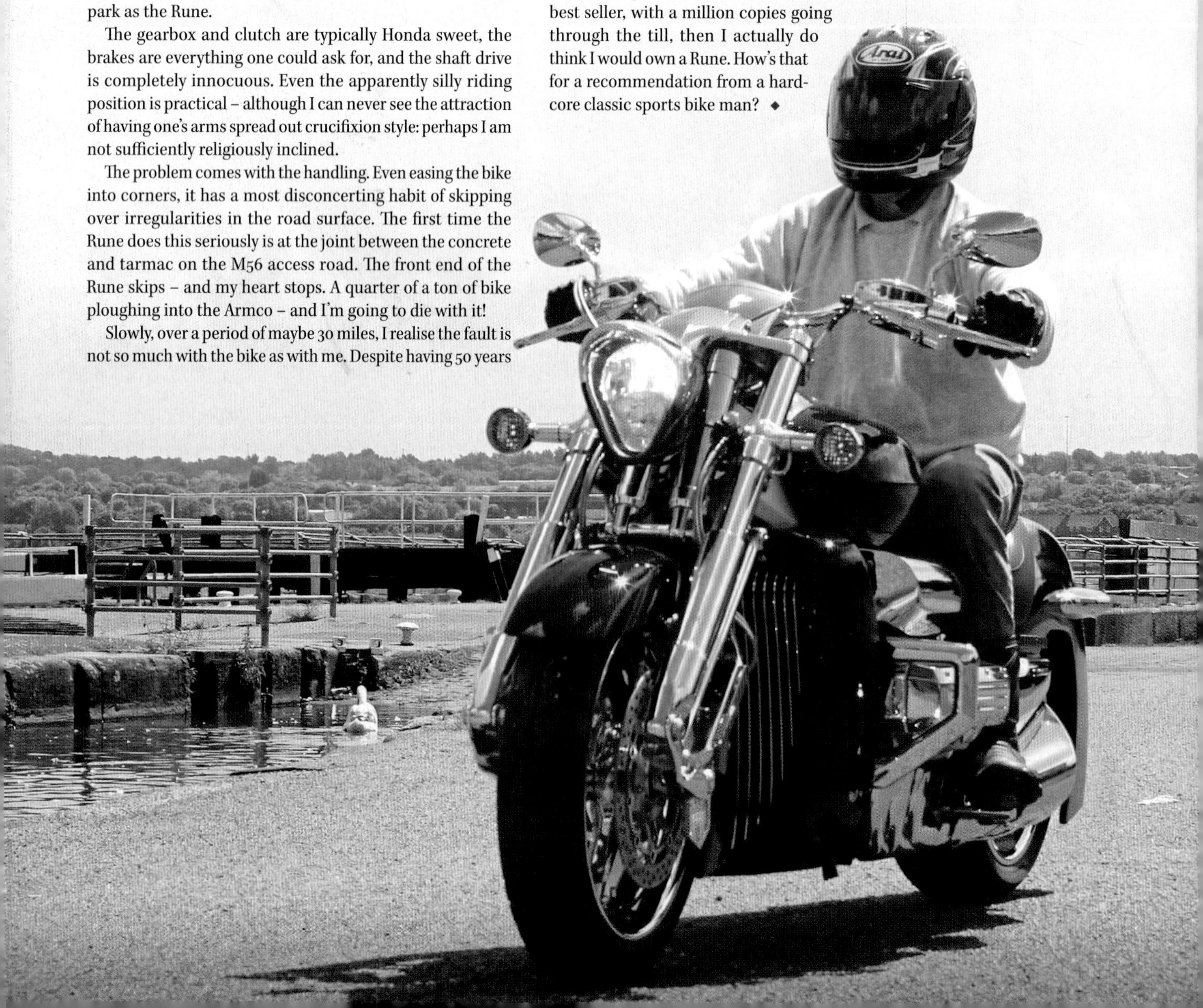